The
Pilates
Pregnancy

Also by Mari Winsor and Mark Laska

The Pilates Powerhouse

The Pilates Pregnancy

A low impact exercise programme for maintaining strength and flexibility

MARI WINSOR with **Mark Laska**

Vermilion
LONDON

First published in 2001 by Perseus Books

This edition first published in the United Kingdom
in 2002 by Vermilion,
an imprint of Ebury Press
Random House, 20 Vauxhall Bridge Road, London SW1V 2SA
www.randomhouse.co.uk
Addresses for companies within The Random House Group Limited can be found at:
www.randomhouse.co.uk/offices.htm

The Random House Group Limited supports The Forest Stewardship
Council (FSC®), the leading international forest certification organisation.
Our books carrying the FSC label are printed on FSC® certified paper.
FSC is the only forest certification scheme endorsed by the leading
environmental organisations, including Greenpeace. Our
paper procurement policy can be found at
www.randomhouse.co.uk/environment

Printed and bound in Great Britain by Clays Ltd, St Ives PLC

The Random House Group Limited Reg. No. 954009

A CIP catalogue record for this book is available from the British Library.

ISBN 0 09 188289 3

CONTENTS

SPECIAL THANKS TO

Mel Berger, Marnie Cochran,
Mark Laska,
and Romana Kryzanowska

This book is dedicated
to the memory of my mother
Ann Winsor-Hanlon

FOREWORD

$\mathscr{I}$ HAVE BEEN DOING Pilates for more than twenty years. Because I have also been a practicing obstetric physician for more than two decades, I have come to believe that Pilates is the best possible method of exercise and relaxation for women who are pregnant.

egnancy much more comfortable and your delivery much easier. Pilates may allow you to decrease your chances of injury before, during, and after delivery and even help your OB-GYN in the delivery room. Pilates may give the baby you are carrying a number of unique benefits as well, and doing Pilates will help you to recover more quickly after your child is born.

Because I am a physician treating pregnant women, I have heard the questions and concerns of hundreds of women who are in your condition. Pilates is the safest possible exercise you can do. But when you are doing Pilates or any other exercise, you have to use common sense: If you feel dizzy, nauseated, or short of breath, you should stop exercising immediately. Exercising when you are pregnant involves some unique considerations. Any time spent flat on your back may cause heart palpitations (as your pregnancy progresses you will notice that this also wakes you up at night); this can be avoided by placing a thin pillow or cushion under one of your hips. But if you do feel palpitations or begin to sweat profusely, stop exercising. If you are directed to assume a position that is too uncomfortable, move on to the next. If that next position causes you discomfort for some reason, stop the routine and begin again in a few hours. Aside from this, nothing that you will be directed to do in this book will cause harm to you or your child in any way.

Pilates offers so many benefits that it is almost impossible to talk about them all. The most unique aspect of this form of exercise concerns circulation. When you exercise to your favorite aerobic videotape or lift weights, your blood travels away from your center and toward the extremities. In other words, blood travels to the body parts that are working and may deprive your child of this much-needed resource. With Pilates, all movements are initiated by your abdominal muscles, and this concentrates circulation within the abdomen, thus giving your child more of what she or he needs rather than less. If this were the only benefit of Pilates, it would be the ideal exercise. But this is only the tip of the iceberg.

With its focus on the abdominal area, Pilates helps those muscles physiologically in a number of ways. Because I have performed C-sections, I have actually seen the difference in the muscular structure of women who use Pilates: Without exception they have firmer, wider, and longer muscles than other women, even women who do many sit-ups each day. During the course of a Pilates exercise, you will perform 500 to 1,000 abdominal exercises that are uniquely designed to develop all four areas of the abdominal muscles. Women who practice Pilates during pregnancy thus not only have fantastic muscle tone but are far less likely to experience muscle separation during delivery. This muscular development in your abdomen will provide better support and will allow your spine to elongate. As your spine elongates, your chest will rise, and these improvements to your posture will give the fetus more room. This will also make you much more comfortable and less susceptible to lower back pain. After delivery, you will feel a sensation like having a hole in your lower stomach area. Because of your strengthened abdominal muscles, this "hole" will feel much smaller than if you did not do Pilates. Pilates is also unique in that it will help you achieve a flatter tummy more quickly after delivery, even if you did not have a flat tummy before you became pregnant. With Pilates you are not creating bulky muscle to show off size. Rather, the strength of the muscle encourages you to step up your activity and improves your coordination and balance, and every day you do Pilates your energy may be enhanced throughout the day.

In addition, Pilates will also teach you to breathe properly, affecting blood flow in your brain and increasing circulation for both you and the child you are carrying. This method of breathing will also help you a great deal during delivery. Pilates is unique in that it strengthens muscles and allows you to become more flexible while at the same time contributing dramatically to your sense of relaxation. During your pregnancy and for your recovery after delivery, the strength and flexibility you gain will be the perfect combination, but knowing how to relax will be an extra benefit.

One of the key issues you will have concerns balance. There are many explanations for your diminishing ability to maintain your balance. The first is the most obvious. Because you will add 25 percent to 30 percent to your total weight over the nine months of your pregnancy, with the majority of that weight around your tummy, your center of gravity will be changing, and changing rapidly. This change can be unnerving. Your sense of balance is instinctual, almost unconscious, but as your pregnancy progresses you will become much more tentative. This tentativeness is compounded by two other factors: the natural hormonal balance taking place within your body and how that hormonal release affects your mental state. A protein called sex-binding globulin regulates how much of each hormone is delivered where and how much of each hormone your body will hold. Pregnant women have relatively more estrogen and less testosterone than usual. Testosterone aids in balance, spatial orientation, and hand-eye coordination. When you do Pilates, your testosterone will rise and this will remedy most of your balance issues.

Let's look at a truly positive by-product of your pregnancy. At this moment you are more motivated to change your life-style for the better than ever before. Men become motivated to positively change their life-styles after they suffer their first heart attack. They begin to watch what they eat, they begin to exercise, they look for ways to reduce their stress, and they become keenly attuned to what is really important in life. During your pregnancy you are becoming aware of the profound significance of giving life, and you are similarly motivated to make sweeping changes. Not only will these changes bring great benefits to your child, but you will be able to build upon these life improvements for the rest of your days. Becoming pregnant may be the single greatest opportunity you will ever have to transform your life for the better.

Like the great majority of the population, most women I treat are not physically active. For those that are, a tiny percentage practice

Pilates. Physical activity can offset some of the discomfort of growing larger. It has been my experience that women who exercise using Pilates find that the added flexibility encourages them to be more active, and they are much more likely to ride a bicycle or go for a walk and to eat properly. This in turn allows them to be more accepting of this temporary new body, and women who are more active and do not binge eat during their pregnancy are more likely to return to their former shape more quickly. Despite the weight gain, the limitations of their new bodies, the decrease in their balance and coordination, women who use Pilates during pregnancy will actually increase their flexibility, and over those nine months they will have a much greater range of motion. They feel much more comfortable in and with their bodies. And when you feel comfortable with your body, you benefit a tremendous amount.

What possible reason could you have *not* to do Pilates? There is no excuse not to do it; all you need is a little space. And it will positively affect your most sensitive issues while you are pregnant. So what do you have to lose? Your baby will have more room inside you. By doing Pilates you may increase circulation to the fetus. You will breathe better, become more relaxed, develop muscle strength, increase your flexibility, expand your range of motion, and become firmer. As a result of all of this, you will move more and move better: You will be likelier to do your normal walking or you will step up your other activities. You will be less likely to have setbacks, and less likely to experience chronic lower back pain. You may have an easier delivery. You will feel more comfortable throughout your entire pregnancy. Pilates is the greatest exercise you can do when you are pregnant, so how could you rob yourself and your baby of these tremendous benefits? In my experience there is only one drawback to Pilates: It can be enormously expensive. But with this book everyone can enjoy the unprecedented benefits Pilates offers. You owe it to yourself to give it a try.

Dr. Uzzi Reiss, OB-GYN

INTRODUCTION

*R*IGHT NOW THERE is a new life growing within you. You are the support system for another being, and the miracle of that process is unfolding before your very eyes each day. This may be one of the most profound experiences in your life. It is a physical, emotional, and spiritual journey into the unknown. This journey will involve bumps in the road, this journey will have physical and emotional pain, and this journey will also include the greatest joy you have ever experienced. That joy will grow each day for the rest of your life.

In every waking moment (and even in some of your nonwaking moments), you will be keenly aware that there is a new life growing inside you. This is a constant reminder that you have a new life ahead of you. Whatever you do and whatever you have done, your life as you know it is changing and will be forever altered by that new life that is inside you. Not only are you making room inside your body to accommodate an embryo, but you are making room in your life for another person. This little person who is growing inside of you is now and will be for some time completely dependent on you. This is a huge responsibility, and that level of responsibility can be daunting, especially if this is your first child. No matter how many children you have, there is always that little voice in the back of your mind saying, "How am I going to do this?" You can read all the books on parenting, you can listen to advice from all of your friends and family, but in the end it is all uncharted territory that you will have to map out.

1

The newness of this experience and all the issues that surround it can be nerve-wracking and sometimes overwhelming. During the nine months of your pregnancy, you will be going through a whirlwind of hormonal, physical, and emotional changes. Especially if this is your first child, these changes can be a shock to your system. Being a hormonal volcano with legs can make you feel more than a little unbalanced, and the hormonal changes are compounded by the physical transformation of your body. This is a time of uncertainty, a time that you may feel out of control. I can rationally assure that all of these feelings and changes are quite natural, yet you *feel* that these changes are quite unnatural to you.

Pilates represents a new tool to use as a coping mechanism in this time of flux. Be assured that for both you and your child Pilates is one of the safest forms of exercise. By doing Pilates regularly, you will provide the best possible physical and emotional environment for you and your child. It is an amazing regimen that will allow you to feel beautiful and graceful and will promote inner calm. Pilates will not only help you during your delivery but will help you to recover more quickly afterward. This method of conditioning will allow you to bring balance back into your life, physically, physiologically, and emotionally. Physically, you will become more flexible, you will have greater strength, and you will become more coordinated than you were before you became pregnant. Physiologically, Pilates will help balance your hormones and promote an inner harmony so that your body is operating at its best and as one efficient unit. Emotionally, Pilates will allow you to feel more in control of your life, more mentally balanced, more open to change and possibility, and better equipped to come at life from a place of strength and assuredness. Using Pilates, you will not only be able to maintain your activity level, your body, and your lifestyle, but over the course of your pregnancy you will improve upon it dramatically.

CHAPTER 1

TOOLS FOR LIFE

*W*HEN YOU BECOME pregnant, you are cast into a sea of hormonal and emotional upheaval. You will find that Pilates is an effective means to deal with and provide sanctuary from this storm. The time you spend doing Pilates is a vacation from the rest of your day, a wondrous activity that promotes calm and clarity, improves the health of your mind, and greatly enhances your inner life. You and your child will not only benefit physically by using Pilates throughout your pregnancy, but you will be able to rely upon Pilates as a means to relieve stress throughout your entire life.

We are all under stress. It is a basic reality of modern life. We have busier schedules. We fit more into our days. We have social and family responsibilities. Our time is stretched and pulled to the breaking point. As women, even under the most traditional circumstances, we are pushed to have it all. More women are part of the workforce, more families depend on our second income, and more pressure is thrust upon us now than has been at any other time in history. We are more responsible, more accountable, more actively involved in our world than ever before. For working women, the luxury (if you can call it that) of becoming pregnant further complicates the demands of life. During your pregnancy there will be stressful issues that come up. Whether it is taking a short sabbatical from the company you started or finding the time to put the finishing touches on the nursery, you will find that there are always (prepregnancy) stresses that you will have to deal with as well as others that will take your stress level even higher.

Your first priority during your pregnancy will be to relieve the stress as much as possible. When you become pregnant, your hormonal levels change. One of the more harmful hormones we have is called cortisol. During pregnancy the levels of this hormone rise, and that in itself will make you experience the effects of stress more deeply. Cortisol, nicknamed "the death hormone," causes many physical illnesses and even more psychological discomfort. With cortisol levels unnaturally high and any stress causing them to rise higher, the physical and emotional danger to you is increased significantly. Every hormonal change that happens within your body also happens within the body of your child. As your cortisol levels rise, so do the cortisol levels of your child. There have been numerous studies that focus on children who are exposed to abnormally high cortisol levels during gestation. These studies show that these children tend to carry higher cortisol levels throughout their lives. Not only does this make them loud and aggressive toddlers and adolescents, but it also predisposes them to and increases their risk of heart disease, diabetes, and cancer as adults. With this knowledge, you should decide to make it an even greater priority to reduce your stress and consequently your cortisol level during your pregnancy.

How do you normally relieve stress? The sad fact is that most of us have a vice that helps get us through our days. Often these are harmful habits. When you become pregnant, naturally you will want to eliminate any bad habits you might have. If you are a smoker, you stop smoking. If you drink or do drugs to cope with stress, you quit drinking or medicating yourself. It is just something that you do. You want to make these adjustments for the health and well-being of the child you are carrying. If you are a smoker, becoming pregnant turns you into a nonsmoker overnight. You automatically cease social drinking and drinking to take the edge off. You no longer rely on antianxiety medications. You immediately remove these bad habits, these "relaxants," from your life. It is not a process but rather an abrupt, cold turkey approach. Under normal circumstances, removing these crutches from your life will have a tendency to make you more edgy, ill at ease, and uncomfortable. During pregnancy, because of the hormonal changes involved, these feelings are heightened and intensified.

Even if you do not smoke, drink, or take medication, becoming pregnant will demand that you create some new tools to cope with life's stresses. Women who exercise as a means to relieve stress will soon discover that they can no longer exercise at levels they are used to. Women who turn to work as a way to relieve stress will find that they cannot maintain the same hours and the same intensity. Basically, everything that we have done, everything that we know how to do, everything that has gotten us through the day up to this point is no longer an effective solution. So what can you do to relieve stress? It has been my experience that Pilates is the ultimate answer.

Before you learn how to do Pilates, I would like to talk about what it can do for you in the context of stress management. First, Pilates is extremely healthy. During pregnancy the most immediate benefit will be an overwhelming feeling of stress relief. An almost magical calm will wash over you as you complete your first session. No matter what level your proficiency, regardless of whether you are performing the first-, second-, or third-trimester workout, whether you have never done Pilates or have been doing it for years, you will receive this tremendous benefit. The reason for this calming effect is primarily a rebalancing of your hormonal levels. Physiologically, hormone levels, especially the level of the stress hormone cortisol, balance out. After completing Pilates exercise, your cortisol level drops significantly—so significantly, in fact, that it will be below normal prepregnancy levels. For you, this essentially means that you will be calmer, more able to cope with responsibilities and whatever comes your way. For your child, it provides an ideal environment, free of stress-causing hormones and the unhealthful effects of that stress. The positive health benefits will both be an advantage before birth and last throughout your child's life.

Although no studies have been performed on why this drop in cortisol occurs, I assume it is due at least in part to proper breathing. Breathing is essential to life. In the context of Pilates, breathing is a fundamental ingredient to proper form. By breathing in the correct manner, not only will you experience the great mental benefits unique to this form of exercise, but you will also help yourself a great deal in the delivery room. If you are now or have ever been a smoker, you know that you relied on cigarettes to relax you. But the chemical narcotic compound in tobacco, nicotine, is actually a stimulant, so it has nothing to do with making you relaxed. What relaxes the smoker is breathing in deeply and exhaling forcefully. It is a strange concept, because along with the breath, the smoker takes in all that noxious stuff; nonetheless, it is true. What relaxes you is oxygen. Think of a stressful situation. When you really visualize that situation, what is the first physical thing you notice? That's right: Your breathing becomes shallow. When you are out of danger, your breathing becomes more regular. Maybe you take several deep breaths as some sort of unconscious response that lets your conscious mind know that you are safe. Take the expression "Whew." It amounts to vocalizing a forceful exhalation. The unconscious process of breathing is something that will become a most conscious process when you exercise using the Pilates method.

Most but not all women have some difficulty breathing when they are pregnant. Especially in the second and third trimesters, breathing is not that unconscious bodily function; rather, it is something they have to think about because it is not occurring naturally. Some women have a shortness of breath; some women feel their babies stretch and move, and this movement invades their lungs. Whatever the case may be, Pilates will help you to increase your lung capacity and diminish shortness of breath, at the same time creating more room for your baby within your body.

As breathing is fundamental to living, it stands to reason that it is also fundamental in movement. When you are moving, if you somehow forget to breathe or take on a strenuous task and hold your breath, your body has a tendency to tense up. For instance, I have found that failing to warm up properly can stress my body and bring on my asthma. This is the physiological reaction when the muscles are not receiving enough oxygen. When oxygen can reach the muscles, the body has the ability to relax—the muscles elongate, and they are able to stretch. Combining focused movement with breathing is the key to elongating the musculature. The more we can oxygenate and elongate the musculature, the less stress we have within the body. The less stress we have within the body, the more freely we breathe.

You can clearly see the advantages to taking in a full breath, but the exhalation is just as important. When we exhale, we expel non-beneficial gases as well as other toxins stored within the body. To put it a rather crude way, exhaling is almost like flushing a toilet. It is one of the primary ways the human body disposes of what is unhealthy. This full exhalation is what I call "wringing out the lungs." The more fully we can exhale, the more air we can take in. If the lungs were a waterlogged sponge, that sponge would not be able to absorb much more water. If we were to wring that sponge out until it was almost dry, not only would we dispose of the dirty water but that sponge would be able to absorb a great quantity of fresh water. Essentially, the quality of our breath depends on how well we exhale.

In Pilates you are in constant motion. Where and when singers and musicians breathe fuels the music. As a dancer, I have experienced how the breath truly links one movement to the next. In the arts this is said to be "organic," meaning that the work transcends mere notes of music or carefully choreographed movement and enters into the spirit of the performer. The breath allows for the whole being to be involved in the performance and relays the passion of the spirit. If breath can allow performers to be fully involved with their work on many different levels, the same is certainly true of breath as it relates to Pilates. Similarly, you will find that breathing, especially during your delivery, is the constant that links all phases and moments of that magical day.

Bodily coordination is certainly emphasized with Pilates, but truly it is breathing that allows us to achieve our intended goals in terms of movement. When you do any sort of stretching, it is important that you visualize breathing into the affected area. When you do Pilates, breathing into the area you are stretching will help you progress, allow you to go deeper, and eliminate or diminish any discomfort or pain. Think of what this can mean to you during your pregnancy. Learning to breathe into discomfort when the baby moves, when you have muscle spasms and cramps, when you experience contractions, and when you are in labor will allow you to relax. That relaxation will empower your body's natural ability to do what it has to do. The likelihood that you will hyperventilate during labor, that you will become light-headed, that you will injure yourself by pushing, will be drastically decreased. If nothing else, concentration on your breathing will let you shift your focus away from discomfort and onto something else, putting you in control. If your breath is the one and only thing you are in control of, whatever else is happening takes on a life of its own, and you become only a part of that greater event. Instead of fighting pain, becoming tense, and experiencing greater pain, breathing into your discomfort will allow you to cope with the discomfort and allow the parts of your body not affected to relax as much as possible. When you breathe and breathe properly, you are oxygenating your system, getting oxygen to the affected area because of your concentration and visualization. When you oxygenate your muscles, they relax. When your muscles relax, you are less likely to experience discomfort and pain.

It is one thing to be calm. It is another thing to be relaxed. The trick is to be both calm *and* relaxed. Although Pilates may be one of the greatest tools to bring about calm, the process of conscious breathing is the ultimate relaxation tool. It is readily available to you whenever a situation demands it. It will be a constant companion in times of stress. Breathing consciously will reduce cortisol levels and help you to become calm. Breathing consciously will oxygenate your system, allowing the muscles to elongate, and when the muscles elongate, you become relaxed.

People who come into my studio for the first time always comment on what an amazing environment it is. They note how everyone around them is open and joyous. The people in the studio are doing Pilates, which many of my clients liken to a drug. It gives them a feeling of euphoria, a high of sorts. They become calm and relaxed. And when people are calm and relaxed, they take everything that life has to throw at them in stride. It doesn't shake them because they are centered within themselves. They are at peace, a deep peacefulness that is within themselves, within their very centers. The combination of becoming calm, becoming relaxed, becoming peaceful allows people to experience joy. It is my belief that joy is the greatest tool that we could possibly have in this life.

CHAPTER

2

THE JOY
OF MOVEMENT

*A*LL RIGHT, LET'S cut to the chase. You have one major concern right now: Being pregnant has completely changed your body. You may not feel as beautiful, you may feel clumsy, you may feel bulky, and you may feel downright *big*. There is a better way to spend your energy than cultivating such feelings. It is time to change your self-perception. You can completely turn around your perception that you are unattractive, clumsy, bulky, and big by finding an exercise regimen that reinforces grace, develops balance and control, is aesthetically lovely when you perform it, and makes you get in touch with how beautiful you really are.

This is a time of great joy for you. This is only a temporary state and you are in a temporary body. But you are at a crossroads. What you do right now, and I mean today, will definitely have a positive effect on how quickly you will recover from your delivery and how fast you will return to your former self—or an even better self. For by practicing Pilates during your pregnancy, you have the opportunity to be in finer physical condition after your pregnancy than you were before you became pregnant.

I get to spend my life helping people transform their bodies and their lives. They do it. They do it all the time. I'm going to help you do it, too. The first life lesson Pilates provides is to accept yourself and love yourself. You need to find the joy of moving. Then you can find the joy of you.

The message of this book is that you have to move. Exercise. Do something. You are very clear about what you could and should be doing because your doctor has given you a prescription for exercise. Pilates will not only help you when you exercise by making you more flexible and more coordinated, increasing your energy, and helping you become more resilient, but Pilates will also help to get you into the mindset of activity and make you much more likely to do your prescribed exercise. You should not see Pilates as a be-all and end-all to your exercise regimen. Instead, you should view it as a most helpful addition to the regimen your doctor has prescribed or to what you normally do.

If you have been very active—if you go to the gym three or four days a week, lift weights, do Tae Bo videos at home, or take several spinning classes a week—the truth is that you will have to slow down considerably during your pregnancy. By practicing Pilates, in addition to a regular and easy aerobic activity (like walking or swimming), you will maintain all of your lean muscle mass. If you are not active, now is the time to get started. Becoming active has a snowball effect. If you begin by doing something like Pilates, you will find that a certain momentum builds. The more you exercise, the more active you will feel. The more active you feel, the more activities you can take on. The more activities you take on, the less likely you are to feel big and bulky. The stronger your self-image, the more comfortable you will feel inside this temporary body.

If you have not been particularly active in the past, increasing your activity level may be difficult at first. You will just have to push yourself to do your prescribed exercises. But when you are doing Pilates, there is no way you will stop your session after completing the first ten minutes. In no time at all you will begin to look forward to your Pilates time.

The pride you take in the physical is what I call "everyday pride." The efforts you make to improve your physical being lead to a sense of self-assuredness, an ability to be comfortable with who you are, and inspire confidence that by doing your best at overcoming and improving various physical obstacles and limitations, you are capable of overcoming anything. No matter how you feel at this very moment, no matter how big you feel, no matter how bulky, now matter how uncoordinated, no matter how cumbersome or clumsy, the pride you take in your physicality and the physiological benefits Pilates offers to you will completely change how you feel, how you move, and consequently how you feel inside your temporary body.

BALANCE

In this book I discuss balance on many different levels: in terms of literal balance, as in not falling down, as well as a balance of muscular structure between a strong side and a weak side of the body. "Balance," however, has a much deeper meaning in terms of its pertinence to your mental state and in your everyday life.

When you become pregnant, literal balance becomes an issue. Pilates can both offset this physical imbalance and prevent injuries because of it. When women become pregnant, they typically gain an additional 25 percent to 30 percent of their usual weight. Unlike a normal weight gain, where those extra pounds would be spread fairly evenly throughout your body, weight gain during pregnancy is all in your belly. This in itself throws off your balance a great deal. In addition to upsetting your balance, the weight gain means a greater threat of injury.

When you increase in size and weight in your abdomen, you have a tendency to sway your lower back, and this causes discomfort and in extreme cases constant pain or even injury. If you injure your lower back, how will you get relief? Your doctor will not give you an injection or prescribe drugs for your pain. Alternative medicine will also be limited. What chiropractor will work on a pregnant woman? Your pregnancy limits what a physical therapist can do for you. You are essentially left to your own devices. Pilates will allow you to elongate the spine and to strengthen your abdominal muscles. The strengthened abdominal muscles, dubbed "the girdle of strength" by Joseph Pilates, will improve your posture, allow the spine to straighten, and dramatically offset your imbalance due to your added frontal weight.

In addition to affecting your physical balance, your pregnancy is also causing an imbalance of hormones. In the previous chapter I discussed the elevation of cortisol levels. Again, while this hormone is at work, its effects are compounded by a decrease in testosterone and an increase in estrogen. Nature intends for you to slow down when you are pregnant. The natural increase in cortisol increases our fear or tentativeness in movement. We are chemically placed in a protective mode. We become uncomfortable around strangers, among crowds, and in unfamiliar places. Testosterone is a major player in hand-eye coordination as well as balance. Even before pregnancy, women have lower levels of testosterone than men do (which may explain the number of women who walk the high wire or drive race cars), but when they become pregnant their testosterone levels decrease even further. So in addition to becoming more protective and tentative, pregnant women have a diminished capacity for balance. The result is that each step they take is unsure or feels unnatural, and they have a greater possibility of bringing harm to themselves and to their unborn children. When men fall, they have the innate ability to break their fall with their hands, but when women fall, they tend to land like logs. Obviously, falling during pregnancy can be problematic. When you do Pilates, however, not only does your cortisol level drop significantly, but there is also a notable rise in your testosterone level. By raising your testosterone levels and decreasing your cortisol level, you will become much more confident in your movement, you will have better balance, and you will both eliminate the sensation of being ungainly and lower your propensity for injury.

Another level of balance, a figurative definition, refers to a big-picture notion of our lives as a whole. If this is your first child, you will be amazed at how much in your life will need balancing over the coming months and years. You will have to balance the immediate needs of your child and your own needs. You will have to balance time between what you normally do and the additional tasks you need to perform as a parent. Soon you will need to balance time between your child and your mate. After a while you may have to balance time between work and your family. You have to balance your energy between those you love and the things you love to do.

Balance can be more general. We need a balanced diet. We balance our attentions between our own interests and what may be good for those around us. Make no mistake: When we achieve physical balance, we do achieve a sense of beauty. Nature likes nothing more than symmetry, and when we attain physical symmetry we become more beautiful in the eyes of the beholder. But balance in one's life is infinitely more beautiful. Balance brings with it a natural harmony, both within ourselves and in the world around us.

When we think about balance in our lives, our primary concern is almost always time. Most people never take time for themselves. They do and do and do for everyone else in the world, but when it comes time for them to do something for themselves, they are either too tired or they have simply run out of time. But *you* have to take some time for *yourself* every day! Take a productive hour to improve yourself. If you think that this is negative in any way, turn it around a little. If you commit yourself to Pilates and it makes you feel great, you are much more capable of making those around you feel great. You will be much more effective at everything you do. Having this balance in your life gives it quality. You will find the room and, more important, the *time* to do everything that you enjoy. When you perform this routine, you enjoy the benefits of self-confidence, pride in yourself, readiness for challenge, and clearheadedness. That mental clarity helps you to be much more productive with your time.

If we make time to work on our physical beings, that time helps us to truly be in the moment. When we live in the moment, we are not ruled by the past, nor are we looking beyond the here and now for what is coming next. We take it all in stride. Being present helps us to be better listeners, to have a deeper understanding of our present situation and surroundings. We become more perceptive and intuitive. We are more successful at work and at home. We are better spouses, better mothers, better friends, and better people when we are really, truly present.

This work allows you to make informed and rational decisions. It allows you to be centered and grounded, so that you are more effective, focused, and clear. It allows you to have a deeper understanding of your surroundings because you are calm inside and without distraction. It allows you to be ready for whatever challenges may come your way. It allows you to operate on a higher level of consciousness.

Although Pilates exercise will take up only a small portion of your day, that brief time will immeasurably enrich your life. Time spent doing Pilates will make you a much more effective parent. It will help you to be more patient with your newborn. It will boost your energy so that any sleep deprivation you experience will be lessened. It will give you a sense of normalcy and centeredness so that you can thoroughly enjoy yourself and the changes you are going through.

With each trimester of your pregnancy, you will pass through several levels of this work, which will lead you to greater and greater rewards. The first stage will be the most difficult. If you have never done Pilates, you will probably note that you have an area that you need to work on. If you have been doing Pilates for years, you may recognize that becoming pregnant has made some of the positions very challenging. This recognition is a critical point in your physical and mental transformation.

We, especially in today's American culture, have an unhealthy definition of "uncomfortable." In our society we value comfort above everything else, and we demand comfort immediately. We view discomfort as something that should be avoided like the plague. But when we avoid discomfort, we also avoid the opportunity to grow. In social or work environments, we can learn to push our own comfort envelope. Each time we test this boundary, our definition of what is comfortable expands, helping us achieve greater and greater goals and making us stronger, more self-reliant, more confident, and vastly more capable.

When you can physically conquer the limitations of your body, and of your body during pregnancy, everything in life gets easier. You become more comfortable inside your own skin. You enjoy being yourself just a little bit more. You enjoy being pregnant just a little bit more. You accept your limitations at this moment and look forward to improving. When we love other people, we love them for their strengths and their weaknesses. With self-acceptance, we can learn to love ourselves.

As you can clearly see, the quality of your life during pregnancy can be greatly enhanced through Pilates. This may involve uncharted territory or may be exactly what you were seeking. If we had not mentioned these wonderful attributes, you may not have been conscious of the changes in your persona. You may not have realized that Pilates helped you achieve these changes, or you may never have realized that improving these areas of your life was in fact the goal of the exercise.

The mental and physiological benefits of this work can be derived only by the quality of your movement. The notion of quality here is much like that implied when you speak of quality time with your spouse or child: It means truly being the best that you can be at that particular time. Quality of movement incorporates being in control, being aware of everything going on inside your body, and being keenly aware of where you are. Your quality of life will be improved by the quality of your movement when doing Pilates. You will enhance the quality of your movement as you concentrate on how each movement flows into the next movement. The transitions are to be very smooth. If you happen to feel a bit awkward, it's okay. Don't be overly critical of your work. Don't worry about doing something wrong. Just move through the routine. If you make little mistakes, you make little mistakes. If you become too uncomfortable, simply modify the exercise so you can continue the movement. But the continuation and the fluidity of the movement are the most important things. They are the key to incorporating quality into the movement. You are trying to capture the joy of movement, and with this particular technique the joy is in the fluidity.

When I first started this routine, I did not get the mental benefits. My movements were mechanical, and I was just going through the motions. But I was quickly able to glean the science behind the movement as I learned the profound importance of having every part of your body working in unison. Like learning a dance step from footprints painted on the floor, I can coach you on what to do and where to move next. Soon after you learn the basic steps, the movements you perform will begin to inform and teach you about the deeper meaning of Pilates. When this occurs, you will become your own coach. As the coach of your body, you must be connected to and aware of every individual piece of the puzzle. I want you to experience your body as a single mechanism working for you.

Understanding the harmony of this routine will allow you to experience joy. To know that all the moving parts of your mechanism are working together as one is an amazing and wondrous experience. It allows you to feel the miracle taking place within. When you are at peace with yourself and when your entire body is working in harmony, you will experience joy. That is the joy of movement. That is the joy of being you.

CHAPTER

3

THE PRINCIPLES
OF PILATES

*T*HERE ARE MANY reasons to do Pilates when you are pregnant. More than any other exercise, Pilates will not draw your blood flow away from your child. Pilates can help you relax and become calm. Practicing Pilates during pregnancy aids you to regain your sense of balance. Pilates gives you a greater range of motion; it builds up your strength while making you more flexible. Pilates increases the surface area of your abdomen by lengthening your spine, creating more room for your child within your body. Pilates lets you be more in control of your life and better equipped to deal with whatever comes your way. But more than anything else, Pilates will allow you to feel more comfortable in this temporary body. When you are in discomfort, you are much more likely not to make any physical move that could possibly make you more uncomfortable. Pilates will make you feel so expansive, so buoyant, so energized, that you will find yourself moving all the time. You will find joy and exhilaration in activity, and your raised activity level will help you a great deal when you shed this temporary body and make the transition back to your normal body.

To experience what I refer to as the joy of movement—to derive all the benefits Pilates offers you—it is important to be aware that there are certain scientific principles at work. Some learn these principles in a logical, linear fashion; some absorb meaning on a more abstract, intuitive level; and others learn by way of the body's informing them, by performing the exercises over and over again. In whatever manner you derive understanding, it is important that you know the fundamentals of Pilates.

The principles of this form of exercise are easy enough to comprehend. Basically, Pilates is a series of exercises or poses that are connected to strengthen then stretch a specific area of your body. As a whole, the routine brings the body into a state of harmony, so that all these different areas are working together as one unit. Unlike most kinds of exercise, Pilates is not about how much, how strong, and how many; rather, it is a sense of the whole body's working in unison that is the goal. Your entire system will be pushed to operate more effectively and efficiently. During your pregnancy, this will have a limitless list of benefits for you and the child you are carrying.

You are to be present for this exercise. Don't leave your brain in the locker room. Yes, you will be performing a very specific routine; however, it is what you bring to this routine that makes this method valuable. As I stated in the previous chapter, you are creating a certain level of quality in your life by partaking in this form of exercise, and to achieve that quality requires your full participation. There are tools that you bring to the physical work of this exercise that will help you to derive its greatest benefits. The tools you will need to have in your workshop are breathing, relaxation, concentration, control, and a heightened sense of fluidity.

BREATHING

As I stated earlier, the goal is for you to become calm and relaxed, and the greatest tool you have to help you reach that goal is breathing. Breathing is a bodily function that we perform whether we are conscious of it or not. The trick is to be very mindful of the manner in which we are breathing. In this form of exercise, each movement is tied to a specific manner of breathing. The breath allows oxygen to nourish the muscles being utilized and to release an array of nonbeneficial chemicals stored in the muscles. These chemicals are related to stress, pain, and fatigue, and they are substances that we are desperately trying to rid ourselves of. To do this requires not only that we take in an ample supply of oxygen but also that we are fully and purposefully exhaling, or what I call wringing out the lungs.

Different disciplines require different methods of breathing. For instance, an opera singer breathes air in below the diaphragm, puffing the stomach out. A musician, especially a woodwind or brass player, breathes into the stomach and proceeds to fill the entire chest cavity and then the throat with air. For this specific form of exercise, it is entirely possible that you will have to retrain yourself to breathe in a new way. When most of us inhale, we expand the tops of our chests. We may think that this is a deep breath, but in fact it is shallow breathing. An extreme example of this is when an asthmatic has an attack. Breathing becomes very labored, and the asthmatic draws air only into the uppermost portion of the lungs in an action that resembles swallowing more than breathing. Instead, you need to learn to breathe into your back, into the area that expands the small ribs. In other words, rather than having your breath expand the front of your chest outward or puff out your stomachs, you should concentrate on filling the bottommost portion of your lungs and get the sensation that you are breathing into the small of your back. This form of deep breathing allows you to bend and move without restricting the amount of oxygen that you are taking in. The oxygen intake allows nourishment to travel to the muscles being worked. As you fully exhale, it allows all of the unused gases and nonbeneficial chemicals stored within your body a route of escape. When you expel these elements, you become more clearheaded, your stamina increases, you release lactic acids within the musculature that make you feel sore, and most important, you become more relaxed.

RELAXATION

One of the skills you will need to learn immediately is how to work out without creating undue tension in areas of your body that are not being worked. When people first begin this exercise, they are simply working too hard. Some people, especially men, have been exercising in a manner that requires brute strength, and often it is the effort put forth that lends the best result. In Pilates just the opposite is true. You will be working a specific area of the body in each separate exercise (believe me, you will know where it is), and as those specific areas are being worked, it is your task to make certain that the areas *not* involved are working to support the movement. When you are riding a horse, there is more to steering than merely sitting on top of the animal and leaving it up to the horse to stay on the trail or not. You are holding the reins, your shoulders are relaxed but ready, your feet are flexed in the stirrup waiting to signal, and you are squeezing with your legs. Your whole body is involved. With Pilates it is the involvement of the entire body that helps to relieve tension in the body. After you finish the routine, you will notice that you have eliminated stress significantly on both the physical and mental levels.

CONCENTRATION

As your ability to concentrate on a particular area of the body improves, you dramatically enhance the quality of your movement. The movements you will be executing are very specific to an area of the body, and it is essential that you concentrate your attention to ensure that that area is working correctly. Often when we move, we are completely unconscious of our action. The brain gets an image of what we want to do, and without really paying attention, the body executes what the brain intended. For instance, there is a significant distinction between lifting up a glass that has been filled to the brim and reaching for your cup of coffee without looking as you read the morning paper. When a brain surgeon is working, you can be fairly certain that any movement that surgeon makes is deliberate and intentional. When we are mindful of our movement, we can employ both the brain and the body to work harmoniously and effectively. Throughout the exercise portion of the book, I not only specify areas of the body that you are concentrating on moving but also suggest some imagery to help you focus.

CONTROL

Control is a key to the quality of your movement. Pilates is not an overly exertive form of exercise; it is specific and intentional movement. You will not be flailing your limbs about here and there; you will be moving with the grace of a dancer, with several parts of your body engaged in mindful movement simultaneously. There are never movements that are propelled by the momentum of throwing a part of the body. The exercise is instead initiated by a stretch and completed by way of contraction or force. When you begin this method of body conditioning, you may go through an awkward stage. The exercises may involve parts of the body that you are not used to moving in unison. Have no fear: Once you have the basic understanding of the movements, you will be able to execute them gracefully—even during the most awkward stages of pregnancy.

WORKING WITHIN THE FRAME OF THE BODY

In Pilates you work inside the frame of your body. When you are standing, your legs are underneath your hips; your arms are underneath your shoulders. Your shoulders and hips "frame" the body. Your joints are supported to a large degree by your smaller muscles. When you work *outside* the frame of your body, it means that your smaller muscles aren't balanced in support of your larger muscles. Once you take the weight of your joint or bone outside the frame of your body, where the frame can no longer support it, then it's on its own. If you are not strong enough to support that movement, you risk injuring yourself.

Most often we see this happen in sports. If you are playing tennis and you swing at a ball that is out of reach, you pull your back. You overextend yourself. Your body does not support the movement, and you get hurt. You can reduce your chances of being injured when you learn to work within the frame of your body, which provides a safe environment for your small and large muscles to work harmoniously without shifting undue weight to your joints. As you become more and more familiar with this boundary, you will be less tentative in your movements and as a result less likely to injure yourself throughout the duration of your pregnancy.

FLUIDITY

To be graceful while you perform this exercise, one movement must seamlessly blend into the next. I think of this whole exercise as being a perfectly choreographed dance, and to perform it with grace means to execute the movements with that precision. Each movement or exercise has a specific point at which it begins and a place where it ends. It is your task for those places to blend into each other and to be unrecognizable points of reference within the whole. Even if you may be instructed to hold at a certain point in each movement for a certain number of counts, that hold is not a place to stop but rather a place where a stretch or movement continues, however unrecognizable it may be to an outside observer. Each exercise leads to the next. There is really no time when the movement stops. The end of one movement is just the beginning of another.

Pilates is an exercise that is paradoxical, or based on premises that may seem to be diametrically opposed. You will be working from the inside out and simultaneously working from the outside in. You will be strengthening smaller muscle groups to support the extra weight you are carrying, to promote the movement and abilities of the larger muscles, and to help prevent injuries. You will be moving in a very controlled fashion to free your mind. You will be using your mind to move the body, and when you are finished with this routine, there will be a closer bond between these two aspects of your being. You will feel whole. Energized. Powerful.

INSIDE OUT/OUTSIDE IN

When you do the routine correctly, you will be using your abdominal muscles, your center, your powerhouse—your inside—as the root of all movement. (This region of the body is so fundamental to the work that I discuss it in detail in the following chapter.) This center is the place that connects the abdominal muscles with the small of the back with the buttocks. From the strength of your powerhouse will emanate dramatic changes in the way you stand, move, walk, carry yourself, and physically relate to the world around you. You will be performing an external movement that will at the same time vastly improve your inner life. It will positively affect your mental clarity, the way you feel, your confidence level, and your energy level, and it will also create a sense of tranquillity and peace of mind.

STRENGTH AND FLEXIBILITY

This work is a combination of art and science. Like a perfectly chore-ographed dance, each movement flows into the next. Each exercise links breathing with strengthening and stretching. Each movement is designed to scientifically oxygenate, then stretch, then strengthen, and then restretch a particular muscle group. The premise of the work is to strengthen smaller muscle groups to support larger mus-cles. When you pick up a barbell to do a set of curls, for example, the object is to isolate your biceps and work them to exhaustion. Pilates, in contrast, develops smaller muscles that would otherwise go unno-ticed. Imagine yourself doing that same curl with the same weight in your hand, only doing it a little bit slower and in a more controlled fashion. You would initiate the motion of your arm from your power-house, and you could now feel that same exercise affect your fore-arm, the shoulder, the scapula, the back, and buttocks, while you used your stomach to support the movement. When the movement is performed in this manner, all of those muscles are working in con-junction with one another. Your body is functioning as a unit. The idea is to achieve your potential results more quickly and without in-jury by using all of the tools available to you.

FREEDOM AND CONTROL

Your added frontal weight during pregnancy may have an adverse ef-fect upon your posture. This makes you particularly susceptible to in-jury. It is imperative that you strengthen your abdominal musculature so that you can support and hold up your spine properly. As you focus on pulling in the powerhouse, the place in your gut that links your stomach with your lower back with your buttocks, you can instantly feel a lengthening sensation in your lower back. In addition, if you pull down the lateral muscles in your back, your shoulders will drop, your neck will lengthen, and your spine will become much straighter. The more you can concentrate on these body parts' working in har-mony with one another, the straighter your spine becomes. Remem-ber the first time someone told you, "Sit up straight"? You probably jutted out your chest, which arches the middle of your back. The key is to pull inward into your spine by using your powerhouse. If you can learn to control this abdominal region of the body and initiate movement from this place, a whole new world of physical movement will be revealed to you. This requires intense concentration.

If you can maintain your concentration and be mindful of the manner in which you are moving, you can experience a peace of mind that is the ultimate freeing experience. To accomplish this you should visualize your body moving through wet cement. This cement does not bind you, and it does not inhibit your breathing, but it does provide resistance, and you have to exert control in order to move. Your movements must not be sporadic or fast. You must at all times maintain control.

Pilates is a series of controlled movements done within the frame of your body so that no movement will pull you from the center of your body. Your goal is always to remain within the frame of your body. The parameters of this frame are marked by the width of your shoulders and hips. You never move your leg out further than where your shoulder ends. If you're lying on your side, you kick your leg forward and back, but you never take it higher than where your hip is. If you exceed these boundaries, you are inviting injury. Get your ligaments and your smaller muscles stronger. Don't rely solely upon the large muscles to lift your leg up, because inevitably you will injure the smaller muscles that support that movement. Always remember to initiate all movement from your powerhouse.

With this exercise there is a routine or structure that will take you through each muscle group. The movements are slow and fluid. This demands that the movements be precise. The precision that this requires takes physical control from your body. As in Tai Chi Chuan, the movements are not jerky but flowing. The movements alternate between stretching and strengthening while you breathe deeply into each pose. As in yoga, the combination of breathing, stretching, and exerting strength has a soothing effect. Unlike yoga, the routine is much more active and nonrepetitive and less likely to lead to boredom. The physical demands of the routine will foster a deep sense of relaxation and a tangible feeling that your daily stress is slipping away effortlessly. It is the precise control that you will demand of your body that will magically free up your mind.

You may experience a renewed creativity and find that spontaneous images pass through your mind while you perform the physical tasks. You may process through the nuances of your day or give birth to a great idea; the pieces to the puzzle may all fall into place. Who knows? While you are engaged in this fluid series of physically demanding exercises, your mind will be free to wander wherever it wants to. This is precisely the mind-body connection you are striving to achieve. This doesn't happen by way of divine inspiration. It occurs by way of a mindful intention to move the body in specific ways.

CHAPTER

4

THE
POWERHOUSE

*T*HE MOST FUNDAMENTAL and essential ingredient to perform this routine is the powerhouse. The powerhouse is located in the center of the body. Your baby is lying right underneath your powerhouse. It is the exact point between the upper half of your body and the lower half of your body, the place between the right side and left side. Anatomically, the powerhouse connects several large groups of muscles: It links the abdomen with the lower back with the buttocks. Joseph Pilates referred to this area as "the girdle of strength." In scientific terminology these muscles are called the rectus abdominis, referring to the oblique muscles, and the transverse abdominis. When you see someone with highly developed abdominal musculature (or "the six-pack," as bodybuilders call it), you are looking at these muscles. The exact musculature referred to as the powerhouse is located beneath these muscles, deeper within the abdomen, and in association with the multifidus muscle is the anchor for the erector spinae group. Where these three muscle groups (the transverse abdominis, the multifidus, and the erector spinae) connect is the powerhouse.

In Pilates all movements are generated by your powerhouse. This is where all of the energy that you exert comes from. Whenever you do an exercise, movement and control over that movement is always initiated by breathing into and pushing from the powerhouse. Always. Before and after pregnancy, most of us who are unhappy with our appearance want to transform this exact area of the body. We want a flatter tummy and a tighter butt. Engaging in this work will bring about those changes by strengthening the powerhouse. Throughout the routine, there is almost constant initiation and use of the powerhouse, and as a result this area will become much stronger and will help to reduce injuries caused by weight distribution during pregnancy and in delivery. For instance, if there's an exercise that requires you to move from your hips, you have to push into your center and initiate the movement from your powerhouse. Otherwise your hips take on the task of moving your entire body, and you can lock up and possibly injure yourself. Pilates may be the only form of exercise that focuses on strengthening this particular region of the body. Because concentration on the powerhouse will increase the blood flow throughout your powerhouse, and consequently the child you are carrying will receive more oxygen and nutrients.

Abdominal muscles crisscross in layers across the front of our bodies like a corset to act as a support for the spine. It is from within the abdominal region of the body, or powerhouse, that we support the spine and all of our major organs. Therefore, when we can strengthen this area, we also dramatically improve our alignment and posture, we can reduce or eliminate many of the problems associated with chronic pain, we can relieve and even reverse conditions that foster back and neck problems, and we may even enhance our overall health. This is especially true during pregnancy, as an increase of strength in this area may help to support your lower back. Adding strength in this area can also help prevent the tearing and ripping of muscles during delivery.

Even if you were not pregnant, the strengthening of the powerhouse would alleviate lower back pain. A lot of people have lower back pain because their centers are not strong and they do not understand how to use their powerhouses. When they attempt to pick up a heavy object or engage in other strenuous activity, they will not call upon their powerhouses to initiate that task. As you strengthen the powerhouse, your bone structure tends to be able to more fully support the weight of your body, which is better prepared to move, to exert itself, and to lift heavy objects. These improvements to your posture will not only help relieve pain but will increase your physical and emotional potential. You will learn that you can rely on this routine to mentally and physically condition yourself. From that center, you can better control your entire life.

It is from the reliance on and strengthening of the powerhouse that you will derive all of the physical, mental, and spiritual benefits of Pilates. The powerhouse is critical to your physical transformation, but it is also essential in developing a higher, more enlightened, self. The powerhouse is the birthplace of us all. Because of it, we humans are the only animals that regularly walk on two legs. The entire evolution of humans required strength in the abdominal musculature to walk upright, and it is this area of our anatomy that allows us to stand erect. In standing erect, humans went through a mental transformation as well. When humans began to walk, they may have been able to process new information or perhaps develop more tools to process that information with. Watch your child closely when she or he begins to walk. You will see that the ability to walk marks a distinct stage of learning. Is it possible that the powerhouse is another communication center for the body? Of course we have large brains, and this enables us to think and process information, but we receive other information as well. We have the senses; we have instinct; we have intuition and perception; we have feelings—information that comes to us on a non-intellectual level. This information comes to us by way of the powerhouse. When we combine the mental and physical sources of information, we as human beings have the unique gift to understand and appreciate our surroundings more fully. The combination of physical and mental information processing just may be why we have the cognitive ability to reason, to emote, to express the profundities of our experience, to ponder the mysteries of our surroundings; perhaps this is why we are the most intelligent form of life on our planet.

When the strength of the powerhouse can adequately support the spine, we begin to strike a balance physically. Along with physical balance, we reap the rewards of balance in many other areas of our lives. To achieve balance is to find a center point. This chapter is specifically about a center point: the powerhouse, your body's center. This is a tangible place that you will become much more attuned to as you participate and grow within this work. Potters begin by centering the clay on the wheel before they create an object. A washing machine that is off-center will shake itself into a malfunction and turn itself off.

When you are playing sports, you can be thrown off balance if you are not centered. And so it is with Pilates. It stands to reason that anything operates better when it's operated from its center. So it is with your body and in your life. Your pregnancy will cause or already has caused a physical imbalance. By practicing Pilates you will develop and rediscover your center in your temporary body.

To be centered is to combine the physical and mental processes. Often there is a distinction between mind and body. Our goal is to have the mental and the physical working in conjunction with one another—to establish a mind-body connection. The brain is the center of all neurological activity and the seat of our intellectual knowledge. The powerhouse is the communication center for the body. Our goal is to be centered, to strike a balance between the mind and the body, as often as we can. It is much like developing a muscle. Being centered helps us to be emotionally available, to be mentally clear, to be capable of accepting challenges, to become more intuitive and perceptive and able to achieve our potential.

That center is the place from which we operate best. That center is the "us" that we love about ourselves. It is the person we wish to be all of the time. That center or powerhouse is the place you speak from. It is where you feel emotional pain. It is where you feel joy and elation. Everything hits you there before your brain has a chance to process the information. The information will eventually transfer to the brain, and you have to force the brain to get the powerhouse to relax; more and more frequently, this will become a winning battle. The more centered I am, the more I pay attention to what's happening to my powerhouse, the better my posture is, the more capable I am in every aspect of my daily life. During your pregnancy, you naturally become more in tune with your center because you tend to concentrate on that area throughout the day. You may already have noticed that regardless of morning sickness or being uncomfortable you feel more solid, more grounded, more in touch, more communicative, more feeling, more compassionate, and more fully alive than you have ever felt. I would contend that you are feeling more powerful precisely because you are more powerfully connected to your powerhouse.

The control that you exert over your powerhouse translates into a calm and clarity from which you can take life's challenges and deal with them appropriately. Over the nine months of pregnancy, you will sometimes feel that you have no control over either your body or your life. After the birth of your child, irregular hours, constant feedings, and the demands that will be placed on you may challenge the notion of control in your own life. There will be many months when you will have to subordinate your own personal needs to the needs of your child. If this happens too frequently, you lose focus. When you are centered mentally, however, you have the strength to care for others more effectively as well as to serve your own interests, and you can allow yourself to enjoy your moment-to-moment life more fully because you are dealing from the truest and purest portion of your being.

As you get more in touch with this physical center, you will become more intuitive. When people say, "I have a gut feeling," they are really not off the mark. This center that you are strengthening allows new information to come in. It is the resting place of instinct. As you develop this area, you will come to trust this more. You will listen to that little voice that is trying to guide you more and more frequently. I have learned that this voice informs daily, and all I need to do is be quiet enough in my center to hear it.

In truth, you are much more in touch with your center, your intuitive self, your powerhouse, than you have ever been before. At this very moment there is a life growing inside of you. With each passing day you become more intimate with that creative energy. This process is nothing short of miraculous, and that miraculous process is all taking place within your powerhouse. As you strengthen your powerhouse during this pregnancy, you will in fact strengthen every aspect of your life. Strengthening this area of your body during this amazing time in your life will allow the concept of *possibility* to enter into your mind and your spirit and your life. Just as the child you are carrying could grow up to be a remarkable person and has the possibility to achieve anything, the journey of discovery that Pilates provides you may have a similar effect in terms of your own personal growth. People say that when they really get into Pilates, it changes their lives completely. Better things come to them. They have greater expectations. They are motivated to do things that they want to do. They are true to their ideals. They can express themselves more honestly. They are more effective at communicating and in their professions. They have fuller, more satisfying personal relationships. The beauty of this form of exercise is that each segment is intended to strengthen your powerhouse. Each time you perform this routine, a new element will be revealed to you, and as a result Pilates will never become boring or repetitive. If this routine becomes your exercise of choice, you will look upon it not as a workout but as a life-style that will continually transform the physical, mental, emotional, and spiritual aspects of your life. When you can find your center and learn to control it, this work, and really everything else in your life, will become much easier to handle.

CHAPTER 5

BEFORE
YOU BEGIN

*I*N THIS BOOK you will find three different workouts that you can use in your first, second, and third trimesters of pregnancy. If you are new to Pilates, I strongly suggest that you advance a trimester. In other words, if you are in your first trimester but have not done Pilates before, begin with the *second* trimester workout. If you are in your second trimester but have not done Pilates before, begin with the *third* trimester workout.

Before you begin, there are a few things you should place in the back of your mind. When you become pregnant, you become more in tune with your body. When your body talks to you, it is essential that you listen and listen carefully. By doing Pilates, the conversation you have with your body will be greatly enhanced. If you ever feel you need to stop, by all means stop. Give yourself permission to do whatever your body suggests.

It is possible, although highly unlikely, that you may become uncomfortable during your sessions. My coauthor became nauseous when he began doing Pilates and discovered that he had scoliosis. This condition in his back made this form of exercise uncomfortable until he learned to adjust his body to accommodate the exercises. Because you are pregnant, your body is different than it has been before. Chances are that you will experience no strange sensations while using this exercise, but if you do, please reread the Foreword in this book by Dr. Uzzi Reiss. It is the best medical advice that can be offered under these circumstances.

The purpose of this book is to replicate as closely as possible the experience of having your own personal Pilates instructor. Throughout the remainder of this book, I take you through the Pilates exercises that are most appropriate for the pregnant woman. I have been a Pilates instructor for over twenty years and have worked with hundreds of women who greatly benefited from this form of exercise during their pregnancies. Because this is a book, and an actual instructor is not at your side, learning the method will be a little unusual at first. If you have never done Pilates before, it would be most helpful for you to read through the instructions and look over the photographs first, then attempt the exercise. I suggest reviewing the instructions each time you perform an individual exercise for at least the first two weeks or so. This may take you out of the flow and reduce the fluidity of the routine as a whole, but in no time at all you will be learning subtle nuances and blending one move into the next. It is a fairly easy learning curve, and once you understand where you are and what comes next, you will become quite proficient. By the time you deliver, you will be well on your way to mastery. I have been doing Pilates for a very long time, and each time I perform it, I am amazed that I learn something new, that my understanding of this form of exercise deepens. Each time I do it, I feel better than before I started. I have found this method to be one of the single greatest gifts I have ever received. It is the gift I give to myself every day. It is one of the most precious and cherished of my possessions. I pass it on to you, hoping that it will become a daily treasure.

No matter how big you feel right now,
No matter how uncoordinated you might think you are
or how insecure about your body you are,
All of that is about to change.

How do you judge improvement when you exercise? If you lift weights, it is all about how much and how many times you can move the weight. If you run, it is all about how fast or how far. Doing Pilates, and doing it properly, is about going someplace you've never gone before in exercise. Doing Pilates properly is about awareness. There are several areas of the body that you should be mindful of as you begin this routine. You will be developing your abdominal musculature and learning the correct placement of your rib cage. You will be developing smaller muscles that you may not even be aware of right now that will better support the movement and usage of your large muscle groups. You will become keenly aware of the tempo and flow of the routine, how one movement blends into the next. You will learn about warming up your body. In doing this series of exercises, you will become aware that whatever your body needs most, you will feel first. Most important, you will learn how to keep yourself motivated so that you can benefit from all the life-changing attributes associated with this method of body conditioning.

When you are performing this routine, it is important that you frequently remind yourself of the importance of the powerhouse. As your pregnancy progresses, it may become difficult to forget your powerhouse. The more frontal weight you have, the more important it is to get in touch with the place that connects the abdomen with the lower back and the buttocks. This routine is all about strengthening and using this specific area. In Pilates all movement and control comes from this area. Remember, it's not just about doing crunches and getting your stomach flat. It's about using your powerhouse to support your new body, and using the powerhouse to initiate and support all movement. It's about getting in touch with your center. It's about getting in touch with a new sense of balance. It's about supporting yourself literally and figuratively.

As you strengthen the abdominal region, another piece of the puzzle fits into place, and that is the proper position of the rib cage. As you transition from the second to your third trimester, proper placement of your rib cage will not only give your child more room but will also help you to breathe, especially when your child seems to be practicing judo or swimming the backstroke. If you feel as if your ribs are protruding, softly, with your breath, let them fall toward your back. By doing this you will lengthen your spine and will feel more properly aligned. Another primary concern of proper rib placement is the area where the ribs meet the sternum. Underneath the sternum lies the uppermost portion of the abdominal musculature, and it is this vital area that is largely responsible for maintaining tension within the powerhouse, as well as being the key in your mastery over the control of movement.

When you do Pilates during pregnancy, you will develop the abdominal musculature. As a result of this work, you may well have a flatter tummy after delivery than you had before you became pregnant. But the primary reason for strengthening these abdominal muscles is to create a more efficient support system for the spinal column and your new body. As this support system strengthens, you can go to work on lengthening the spine itself. The elongation of the spine is critical to doing this work correctly and deriving many of this routine's great benefits. The longer your spine is, the more efficiently your body operates. The more efficiently your body operates, the more efficiently your nervous system operates. The more efficiently your nervous system operates, the more efficiently your blood flows. The better your circulation, the healthier the environment for your child. The longer your spine is, the more room for your child. The longer your spine, the more room you have between vertebrae. Energy passes through the vertebrae all along the spine. The more space between your vertebra, the more energy you will have. Try it the next time you feel yourself getting tired. There you are, your shoulders rounded, slouching in your chair. The spine is collapsing. Now take a seat on the floor with your legs crossed and keep lengthening your spine. Close your eyes for five minutes. Feel yourself getting taller as each vertebra lifts itself above the one below. The spine is the only set of bones in your body that you can work on to improve your posture and actually become taller. Lengthening your spine is essential for creating the optimum environment for the fetus and transforming the way you look and feel.

If you have never done Pilates, soon you will be working some of the smaller muscles that you are not used to working. If you have ever taken up a new sport, you have probably said, "I feel like I used muscles that I didn't know were there." So it is with this. Even if you exercise regularly, these are not muscles that most people pay close attention to. As you strengthen and develop these muscles, however, you will become much more adept at any physical activity and far less likely to injure yourself.

A prime example of where smaller musculature supports large musculature—and a location people are most prone to injure—is the knee. The knee is one of the weakest joints in the body. There are a great many muscles that support its proper placement, and there are several ligaments that allow it to move in the way it was designed to move. When you say, "I threw my knee out," the pain you feel may not even be in your knee; it is more likely that the pain is coming from the smaller muscles that keep your knee in place. In the case of most injuries, the kneecap slides out of place because the ligaments aren't strong. With Pilates you will be strengthening your quads and your inner and outer thighs so that those muscles will promote proper placement of your ligaments and joints. Small muscles support larger muscles throughout the body, and you will notice that when you do engage in physical activities, you will be much more comfortable and capable. You will have a sensation that everything is connected. You will become aware of your body moving as a whole. You will have a sense that your entire body is working as a single unit, in one coordinated action. You will feel graceful. You will feel beautiful.

When you begin to understand how one move blends into the next, you can start to concentrate on the tempo of the movement as a whole. In Pilates there should be no jerky movements. As I've said before, imagine yourself moving through wet cement. The cement prevents you from moving quickly, putting up resistance. You can't throw your limbs in wet cement; you have to concentrate on how to get from point A to point B. Then you realize that there are thousands of points that you must move through to do so. Notice how wading through this cement creates a certain tension within the muscles. They aren't exactly flexed, but they aren't relaxed either. When you are doing this exercise, make certain that you engage the entire body in this way. Remember, your movement isn't necessarily slow, but it is constant and controlled. This controlled movement should remain within the frame of the body. When you move outside this frame, you become far more likely to injure yourself.

As you begin, you will be keenly aware of the parts of your body that are weak and need to become more flexible. Whatever your body needs most, you will feel first. If you're inflexible, the first thing you feel is more flexible. If you need better motor skills, the first thing you will feel is that you are becoming more coordinated. You will notice a vast improvement in your overall sense of well-being. You will feel an almost spiritual connection to your body. You should feel rejuvenated after only your first workout. You will also feel a drastic reduction in your stress level. When you experience stress, your muscles actually constrict, or tie up in knots around the joint. This leads to backaches, to tightness in the shoulders, headaches, and many other illnesses. One of the aspects of this exercise that you will concentrate most on as a beginner will be to lengthen these muscles away from the joint.

Performing Pilates will also test your will. If I told you that by spending an hour a day three or four times a week, you could become physically fit; that while you are pregnant you could become stronger, more flexible, and have a greater range of motion; if I told you that you could have a better body after delivery than you had before you became pregnant; if I told you that you could prevent, alleviate, and eliminate pain associated with pregnancy, decrease the amount of pain and injury associated with delivery, achieve a keener level of balance than you have ever enjoyed, become more confident, dramatically reduce your stress level, be more calm, be more approachable, become more intuitive, experience elation like you have never felt, give the child you are carrying every possible advantage, and learn to truly love yourself, can you think of anything that would stop you from doing Pilates? Achieving these tremendous benefits will only happen if you show up. It will require some discipline to learn the routine, but you really can do it. Once you have become proficient and understand how to do it, you may still not want to work out, but that will only last for the first ten minutes. I promise to get you through those first ten minutes, but I want you to make the commitment to bring yourself to this work. The more you want to improve your life, the easier you want your pregnancy to be, and the more you want to improve the quality of life for the child you are carrying, the greater and more profound your experience will be. The greater your will, the greater your rewards.

CHAPTER 6

FIRST-TRIMESTER WORKOUT

𝒯HE ONE HUNDRED

> *Through this exercise you are increasing your circulation and warming up your body with a combination of breath and movement. When you are finished, you should feel warmth around the area of your heart.*

PREP

Lie on your back. Feel your whole spine meet the floor. You should have the sensation that your spine is long and open. Your arms are at your sides and long against your body, and your palms are flat on the mat. Your knees are pointed to the ceiling, and your feet are flat on the mat.

READY

Bring your knees into your chest and stretch your legs up at a 90° angle.

Use your powerhouse to bring your chin into your chest and continue that motion as you roll up.

Do *not* lift your upper body higher than the base of your shoulder blades.

Continue to pull your ribs down and press your lower back into the mat.

41

Maintain this necessary support for
your spine.

ACTION

Pull your powerhouse tightly into your
lower back.

Inhale slowly through your nose for five
counts while pumping your arms up
and down. Your arms should be rigid—
think of them as hammers pounding in
nails.

Exhale slowly through your nose for
five counts, continuing to pump your
arms up and down.

Pull in that powerhouse. Keep your
arms straight. Keep only your arms and
shoulders involved in the movement.

Repeat the cycle until you have counted
up to 100.

Now relax completely.

As you become more advanced, you can
gradually lower your legs. As you build
strength in your powerhouse, you can
lower your legs in increments (as long
as your lower back maintains contact
with the mat) until they are at eye level.

$\mathcal{T}$RANSITION

> *As in a dance, transitions between exercises allow us to move from one pose to the next. As you become more proficient, the entire exercise program will be one continuous movement, from beginning to end.*

Hug your knees back into your chest.

Release your legs and place your feet on the floor, with your knees pointed toward the ceiling.

Stretch your legs out so that they are long against the mat.

Bring your arms back up past your ears; your arms should reach straight up from your shoulders.

Bring your legs together.

Feel comfortable within this frame you have established.

Now your body is in the proper position for the next exercise, Roll-Ups.

When you are beginning, you can use either a yardstick, a 3-foot dowel from your closet, or a towel held taut between your hands.

ROLL-UPS

> *This exercise will really put you in touch with your powerhouse and will also give you a nice stretch in your hamstrings and spine. The powerhouse connects everything—from your fingertips down through your toes. As you do this exercise, try to feel that connection.*

READY

Lie flat on your back. Feel that your spine is supported and neutral against the floor.

Relax your ribs. Your legs should be together and flat against the mat. Your arms should be reaching up above your head, no wider than shoulder length apart, with your palms facing upward. Create a space between your shoulders and your ears. Relax your shoulders. Initiate your powerhouse by sinking your navel in toward your spine.

ACTION

While breathing in, raise your arms toward the ceiling.

As you reach for the ceiling, use your powerhouse to bring your chin toward your chest.

44

Keep reaching through your fingertips.

Your ribs should tweeze down into your powerhouse. Imagine that your chin could hold an apple against your chest.

While breathing out, continue reaching with your arms, curling over as your fingers reach toward your toes.

Your spine should not straighten. Maintain a curved position by pulling your navel into your spine. Continue exhaling until you touch your toes.

While breathing in, roll down.

Keep reaching with your arms, keeping them at shoulder level.

Pull your powerhouse into your lower back to maintain the curve in your lower back.

Your lower four vertebrae will make contact with the mat first.

Hold your breath at this point as you continue a controlled curl down, vertebra by vertebra, like a cobra.

Reach with your arms to control your roll down.

Now exhale forcefully as you complete the roll down.

Repeat 6–8 times.

$\int$INGLE LEG CIRCLES

In this exercise you are loosening your hips and stretching your hamstrings. Despite the name of the exercise, try to trace a rounded triangle, an oval, or a football shape using your leg. Keep the motion smooth. Use your powerhouse to support this motion and squeeze your buttocks for support.

READY

Lie flat on your back. Your hands should rest comfortably at your sides.

ACTION

Hug your right knee into your chest.

Keeping your leg aligned with your hip, relax your leg straight up.

Get as close as you comfortably can to forming a right angle with your body.

Now without moving your hips, cross your leg over your body like a windshield wiper.

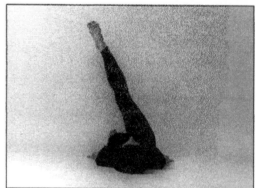

Once your leg has passed your shoulder, swing it down past your passive leg like a sickle by about 6 inches, then up toward the ceiling.

46

Stay within the frame of your body—keep your leg inside the frame of your shoulders.

Now repeat this motion 4 times.

Reverse the movement and repeat 5 times.

Change legs.

Pull your left leg into your chest and extend your right leg out.

Do 5 circles in each direction.

ROLLING LIKE A BALL

This is like a little massage for your back. Your goal for this exercise is to not let your heels touch the floor. You will be coming to a point of balance right on top of your sit bones. Achieving this balance requires control. Do not use your momentum to come back up. Use your powerhouse.

READY

Sit up and bend your knees as you scoot your buttocks toward your heels.

Hug your ankles and curve your spine gently over them.

Bring your chin into your chest.

Maintain this position by pulling your powerhouse into your spine
and curving your back even more, drawing yourself into a ball.

Form a C with your spine.

Arch your feet. Only your toes should be touching the mat.

Maintain this position as you. . .

48

ACTION

Inhale slowly and feel your powerhouse.

Begin rolling back by bringing your navel into your spine.

Exhale slowly.

Use the momentum of your breath to return forward.

Maintain a ball position.

Repeat 6 times.

$\int$INGLE LEG STRETCH

> *This exercise is designed to work on your coordination, relax the hip flexors, and link breath to movement. As you concentrate on your powerhouse while you begin this movement, you will feel your abs strengthening. Keep your shoulders square. The only parts of your body that should move are your arms and legs.*

READY

Lie flat on your back.

Your legs are extended directly out of your hips and relaxed flat against the mat.

Your arms rest against your body, your palms flat on the mat.

ACTION

Inhale slowly. Lift your chin toward your chest.

Use your powerhouse to raise your head and shoulders off the mat.

At the same time, bring your left knee into your chest and your left hand to the outside of your left ankle while placing your right hand atop the inside of your left knee.

Your shoulders should be relaxed, your elbows open.

Relax your ankle. Tug on your leg twice, breathing out as you go.

Now switch legs.

Your outside hand goes to your ankle.

Keep your leg in alignment with your body.

Tug twice and switch.

Contract your powerhouse as you exhale and engage your stomach muscles at all times.

Repeat 5–10 times.

$\mathcal{D}$OUBLE LEG STRETCH

With this exercise you will be folding and unfolding your body. As your powerhouse contracts, you fold. Imagine a comet hitting the earth, sucking everything into the hole its impact leaves on the surface. That's what your body is doing: The comet hits your powerhouse, and you fold in.

READY

Glue your legs together.

Bring your knees in toward your chest and hug your ankles gently.

Use your powerhouse to lift your chin to your chest.

Exhale slowly for three counts and contract your powerhouse further by pressing your belly button toward your spine.

ACTION

As you inhale, lengthen your legs and lift them up to a 45° or 90° angle. Your torso remains fixed.

Bring your arms up straight and long until they are even with your ears.

52

As you exhale, sweep your arms around by your sides.

Using your powerhouse, slowly draw your legs toward your abdomen and hug your ankles.

Hold.

Using your powerhouse, stretch your limbs away from your torso then pull them back in.

Reach. Fold. Hug.

Repeat 5–10 times.

$\mathcal{S}$INGLE STRAIGHT LEG

This exercise is designed to increase flexibility in your legs, especially in your hamstrings, and to strengthen your abs. The straighter your legs, the more you will feel this in your abs.

READY

From the Double Leg Stretch, bring your right leg straight up until it is perpendicular to the mat.

Extend your left leg straight out like an arrow coming out of your hip socket, until it is off the mat at a 45° angle.

ACTION

Inhale as you reach your arms up and place your hands around your ankle if you can. If you can't, place them around your calf or your thigh.

Lift your head, chin to your chest, bringing your shoulders off the mat.

Keep those shoulders pressing down.

Exhale as you stretch your right leg further by tugging it toward you twice—one, two.

Pull in your powerhouse as you switch legs in a scissorslike motion, bringing your left leg up toward your body.

Try not to move your torso.

Exhale as you pulse your left leg twice.

Now add some tempo to the movement. Make it vigorous.

Inhale every 2 sets and exhale every 2 sets.

Repeat at least 10 times.

$\mathscr{D}$OUBLE STRAIGHT LEG

This exercise is designed to build strength and power within your powerhouse. Lower your legs only as far as you can while keeping your lower back on the mat.

READY

After you have completed the Single Straight Leg, bring your hands behind your head. *Do not clasp your hands.* Either put one hand under the other or touch your fingertips. Now rest your head into your hands. Your ribs are pulled down.

Use your powerhouse to bring your chin toward your chest so that your shoulders are off the mat. Both legs are straight up and perpendicular to the mat. Your lower back is pressed against the mat.

ACTION

Inhale as you glue your legs together and move them down slowly toward the floor. Get your legs down as far as you can without bringing your lower back off the mat.

Take two counts to bring your legs down and one count to bring them up.

Your powerhouse guides your legs by contracting down toward the spine as you bring your legs back up.

Repeat 10 times.

56

CRISSCROSS

> *The Crisscross is great for your abs. You should really begin to feel your abs working, especially if you start slowly. As one side of your body contracts, the other is reaching back into a stretch. This oppositional movement works the abs diagonally.*

READY

From the Double Straight Leg, bring both knees into your chest.

Extend your left leg up toward the ceiling, making certain that your lower back is pressed into the mat. Your ankles should be relaxed but not loose. Your head and shoulders should remain off the mat. One hand is over the other behind your head, and your elbows are open and should be extended straight out from your ears.

ACTION

Begin by moving slowly. Breathing in, count one-one thousand, two-one thousand, as you bend your right leg toward the middle of your right collarbone.

Your left leg extends from your hip at a 45° angle.

From the waist, use your powerhouse to twist your torso to the right. Your torso should move as one unit. Look at your right elbow as you place your left elbow inside your right knee.

Hold for two counts.

Switch sides.

Legs straight out from the hips, stay within the frame of your body and repeat 3 more times.

Now double your tempo on the next 4 reps.

The small of your back should be pressed against the floor. Firmly glue your butt to the floor, and don't rock your hips.

Double your tempo again for the next 4 reps.

(Move to the tempo of "God Bless America.")

$\mathcal{S}$PINE STRETCH FORWARD

> *This exercise provides a nice stretch for the entire back and is*
> *great for your posture. You can really create some space between*
> *the vertebrae, resulting in a tactile sensation of lengthening the*
> *spine. The key to performing this exercise correctly is to contract*
> *your powerhouse into your spine, intensifying that contraction*
> *throughout the exercise.*

READY

Sit up. Open your legs a bit wider than
your hips. Push your heels away from
you (i.e., flex your feet). Extend your
arms forward as if you are sleepwalking.
Use your powerhouse to lengthen
your spine.

ACTION

As you inhale, contract your
powerhouse into your spine.

Curve your back as much as you can,
shaping it into the letter C. Keep your
arms in the sleepwalking position.

Maintain the C curve, as if you are
rounding over a beach ball.

Exhale.

Reach your arms forward. Reach the upper portion of your torso forward while maintaining your contraction. Your hipbones should be over your sit bones. Your buttocks should feel as if they are glued to the floor.

Inhale.

Roll back up and sit up tall.

Exhale.

Repeat 3 times.

NECK ROLL

Look slowly to your right, keeping your shoulders down.

Come back to center.

Look slowly to your left.

Repeat.

Tilt your head toward your right shoulder and circle your head around, the crown of your head leading the way, until your left ear is pointed toward your left shoulder.

Reverse the half circle.

Repeat twice.

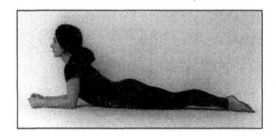

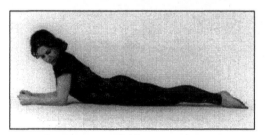

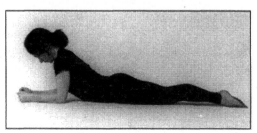

$\int$INGLE LEG KICK

This exercise is great for control, coordination, and flexibility in your upper chest and thighs. This movement is very precise, so use your powerhouse to move your legs. When your legs come up, be careful not to throw them toward your buttocks. When your legs come down, use your powerhouse to provide resistance.

READY

Lie on your stomach and bend your arms. Your elbows should be directly beneath your shoulders, with each hand closed in a fist.

Lift your sternum and chest. Keep your neck long. Your legs should be flat against the mat.

ACTION

While bending your right leg, reach your heel toward your buttocks and pulse twice.

Relax your right leg.

Bending your left leg, reach your heel toward your buttocks and pulse twice.

Use your powerhouse to pull your abs into your spine.

Tighten up your tush.

Be a little bit more vigorous with the movement.

One, two. Don't move your hips.

Now relax your left leg.

Repeat 5 sets.

*L*ITTLE PIECE OF HEAVEN

My mentor, Romana, named this exercise. We have been arching and working the lower back, and now it's time to give that area a little reward. Throughout your session, you may perform this exercise as many times as you wish. If your knees hurt when you are rounded over, simply place a pillow between your buttocks and heels.

READY

You are still lying on your stomach.

ACTION

Use your hands and arms to push yourself back onto your heels until you are kneeling with your back rounded over. Your head is focused toward the mat. Your arms are extended long in front of you.

Push your hips to your heels for a deep lower back stretch.

Doesn't this feel great? Breathe slowly and deeply and rest your back.

$\int$AW

This exercise will stretch your hamstrings and your entire side from your waist up. Keep your buttocks equally and firmly planted on the mat to maximize this stretch. Wring out your lungs when you exhale.

READY

Lift up from your powerhouse and sit up tall. Your legs should be long against the mat, shoulder-length apart, with your kneecaps facing the ceiling.

Extend your arms out to the sides like wings on an airplane, keeping them in your peripheral sight.

Pull your powerhouse into your lower back with your shoulders pressing down toward your lateral muscles (your lats).

ACTION

Exhale as you glue your butt to the floor and use your powerhouse to twist slowly to the right. Twist from your waist, not from your hips.

Reach your left pinky toward your right little toe (your right arm will drop when it gets behind you).

Stretch your body forward over your leg. Relax your neck and keep your opposite hip down.

Exhale slowly as you perform 3 sawlike movements.

Saw that little toe off. Stretch from your waist. Finish exhaling.

From your powerhouse roll up and return to center.

Repeat on your left side.

Repeat 4 sets.

CORKSCREW

> *This exercise is terrific for control as well as flexibility in your spine. There are two levels for this exercise. When you are pregnant, do only the first portion of the exercise when you begin. As you become more proficient, add the second.*

READY

Bring your legs together and roll down to the mat vertebra by vertebra until you are lying flat on your back.

Your arms are straight down by your sides, your palms flat against the mat.

Lift your legs toward the ceiling, with the small of your back pressed against the mat.

ACTION

Glue your legs together.

Initiating from your powerhouse, move your legs to your left in a counterclockwise motion as you use your toes to outline a circle the size of a large pizza.

Inhale at 12:00. Exhale at 6:00.

Now reverse the circle.

Repeat 3 times.

$\mathcal{N}$ECK PULL

This exercise is designed to strengthen your powerhouse and improve your posture. If you can remember to pull your lats down, it will not only make the exercise easier to execute but will provide you with additional length in your spine and ensure proper alignment.

READY

Lie flat on your back. Your ribs should be relaxed, your belly button pressing down into your spine. Touch your fingertips behind your head. Your elbows are pointed away from you.

Pull your lats down so that you have a big space between your shoulders and your ears.

Pull in your powerhouse.

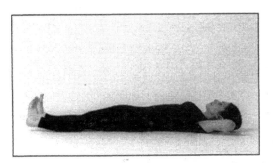

ACTION

Your feet are flexed, and your legs are hip-width apart.

Inhale as you lift up your head and bring your chin to your chest.

Continue rolling up, pulling in your rib cage, and keep reaching with your legs.

Roll over all the way until your elbows are pointed down to the floor.

As you come up, open your elbows to the side and lift up tall.

Lengthen up in the spine. Pull your ribs down. That's it. Now you have a nice tall back.

From here, lean straight back on an angle. Now contract your belly button toward your spine to roll the rest of the way down, lengthening your legs as you go.

Repeat 5 times.

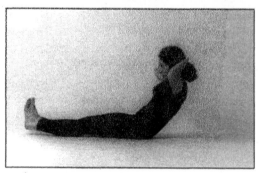

$\int$PINE TWIST

The purpose of this exercise is to improve your posture by loosening your spine and increasing flexibility in your hips and waist. What you are really doing is isolating your waist. To get the most out of this exercise, initiate the movement of twisting only from your waist. You will be watching the hand that is moving. The motion is like sweeping back a circular shower curtain. Don't make the mistake of letting the hand that is moving initiate the motion. You don't want to force the sweeping movement, and you don't want to push it from momentum created by the motion.

READY

Sit up tall with your legs extended straight out from your hips and your arms in the sleepwalking position. Everything is reaching forward. Your torso is high.

Pull down your lats. Your shoulders are relaxed. Your neck is long.

ACTION

As you exhale, slowly twist from your waist to your right.

Stay focused on your right hand and let the movement of your waist twist your torso as one unit. Your left hand remains forward.

Ideally, both hands will be in a straight line when you have completed the twist. Go as far as you comfortably can.

As you inhale, slowly bring your right arm back to the sleepwalking position.

Exhale as you twist to the left.

Switch and repeat.

Repeat 3 sets.

$\mathcal{S}$IDE KICK SERIES

> *The only portion of your body that should move throughout this exercise series is from your hips down. You should use the power-house to hold your torso still and fixed. In this series you will be lying on your side; body positioning is a key element of executing these exercises correctly. Your upper hip must stay directly on top of the other hip. It should not become displaced because of the movement. Your torso should remain straight, long, and strong. This is a great exercise for the buttocks and thighs and also promotes balance and control.*
>
> *Begin on your right side. Go through the entire series, then roll over and go through the series on your left side.*

READY

Lie on your right side. Your bottom arm should be extended straight up from your shoulder.

Your elbow should be bent, your hand supporting your lifted head.

Place your top arm in front of you with your hand flat on the mat for support.

Keep your shoulders down. In the "pike" position your legs extend straight down from your hips, which are stacked on top of one another. Your powerhouse is pulled in, and your lower back is long.

71

Bring both legs, glued together, up and forward about 8–12 inches, so your body forms an angle: From the waist up, you're perfectly straight. From the hips down, you're at an angle.

ACTION

Lift your top leg so it is even with your top hip. Your ankle should be relaxed but not loose.

Bring your leg forward as far as you comfortably can and pulse twice—one, two.

Think of your leg as an arrow coming out of your hip socket.

Keeping your torso fixed, bring your top leg down past your bottom leg and pulse twice to the back—one, two. Your powerhouse moves your leg.

Repeat 10 times.

$\mathcal{B}$ICYCLE FRONT/BACK

READY

Remain on your side with your head propped up by your arm.

Bring your top leg straight out in front of you so your foot is adjacent to your belly button and bend your knee without moving your thigh, keeping your knee hip-level.

ACTION

Take your heel to your buttocks, shifting that shape to the back, and then stretch your leg.

Bring your leg straight front.

Repeat 3 times.

Now reverse the direction for 3 more.

$\mathscr{L}$EG LIFTS

READY

Remain lying on your side with your head propped up.

Your legs should be extended straight down from your hips in a pike position.

Rotate your top leg so your kneecap is facing the ceiling. Now one hip is on top of the other.

ACTION

Lift your top leg up and slowly bring it straight down. Go only as far as your flexibility will allow. Don't force anything. Try not to let your upper hip roll back; keep it right in alignment with your lower hip.

Up and slowly down. And up and slowly down. It's a controlled kick.

And up and slowly down.

Again, your torso stays still, and your stomach is pulled in. Don't forget to breathe.

Ankles are relaxed but not loose.

Repeat 10 times.

$\mathcal{S}$MALL LEG CIRCLES

READY

End the last exercise with your leg extended, on top of the other leg. Think of your leg as an arrow coming out of your hip socket.

ACTION

Moving from the hip, draw a cantaloupe-sized circle with your leg. Try not to make a circle from your knee or ankle.

And reverse. That's it.

Keep your knees straight, use your powerhouse for support, and don't forget to breathe!

Repeat 10 times.

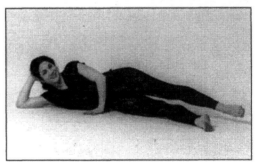

$\mathscr{L}$ARGE CIRCLES

READY

Keeping your torso still, reach forward with your top leg.

ACTION

Draw a big circle with your toes. Completely isolate your top leg, guiding it with your hip by using your powerhouse. Keep your hips and lower leg still. Pull in that powerhouse. Don't let your torso move back and forth. If you're more advanced on these, you can pick up the hand that's on the floor and put it behind the other ear: Then you have to really use your powerhouse for control.

Reverse and repeat 5 times.

*H*OT POTATO

READY

Bring your top leg down.

ACTION

Lift your top leg, bring it about 6 inches in front of your bottom leg, and tap it on the floor twice.

Making a half circle, move your top leg 6 inches in back of your bottom leg and tap it on the floor 3 times.

Add some more dynamics. Move your leg to the tempo of "God Bless America."

Repeat 10 times on each side.

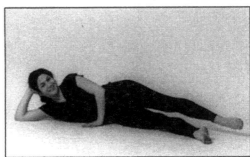

$\mathcal{S}$CISSORS

READY

You are still lying on your side with your head propped up on your hand.

Lift both legs about 6 inches above the mat, or as far as you comfortably can.

Don't roll your hips to the back; stack your legs on top of one another.

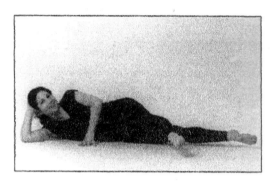

ACTION

One leg moves to the front as the other moves to the back.

Now switch, just like a pair of scissors. The movement is fluid and balanced.

Pick up the tempo. Big movement.

Give yourself some space between the ankles. That's it.

Your powerhouse should be pushing in toward your spine.

Repeat 10 times.

Now roll onto your other side and complete this series for that side.

$\mathscr{L}$EG LIFTS

> *This series of four positions is not from traditional Pilates exercises but is of my own design. I find these leg lifts a fantastic continuation of the Side Kick Series and a way to work the thighs even more. For best results, pretend your legs are moving through wet cement. The closer the cement is to drying, the more resistance your movements will meet.*

READY

After the Scissors, bring your knees up, one leg directly on top of the other.

ACTION

Lift your top leg no higher than your hip. Release that leg down slowly into your starting position.

Repeat 20 times.

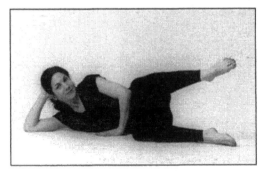

Turn your knee down so it is touching the opposite knee. Lift your leg. Now slowly bring it back into your starting position.

Repeat 20 times.

Bend your knees. Bring your feet together. Open and close your legs like a clam.

Repeat 20 times.

Draw a circle with your knee—forward, up, down, together.

Repeat 10 times clockwise and 10 times counterclockwise.

**GO BACK TO PAGE 71
AND REPEAT THE ENTIRE SERIES
WITH THE OTHER LEG.**

$\mathcal{T}$HE ASTRONAUT

> *The starting position for this exercise is similar to the Modified Roll-Up starting position. This exercise will help you strengthen various muscles that are used during delivery. If you feel cramping or pulling at any time, stop the exercise immediately.*

READY

Start in a sitting position with the bottoms of your feet flat against the floor and your hands underneath the backs of your thighs.

Round your back and tighten your buttocks for additional support.

ACTION

Slowly release your arms forward and hold for a count of five.

Place your hands back under your thighs and rest for five counts.

Release your arms back into the starting position.

Repeat 2 more times.

$\mathcal{K}$NEELING SIDE KICKS

TRANSITION

Bring your right knee underneath you, then the left.

Kneel and come up to center. You want to be completely straight, with your pelvis pushing forward. You don't want your buttocks to be sticking out at all.

Stretch out your sides a little before you begin.

Standing straight up on your knees, drop your right hand toward the mat and feel the stretch in your left ribs.

Come back to center.

Drop your left hand toward the mat and feel the stretch in your right ribs.

READY

Lean to your left. Let your left hand keep you from falling by placing it directly under your shoulder. Your left hip is directly over your left knee.

Extend your right leg to the side so it is parallel with the mat.

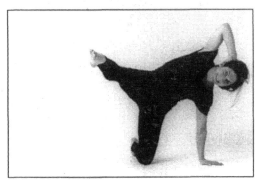

Your head should stay in the middle of your shoulder blades.

Place your right hand behind your head, pulling your elbow back as far as you comfortably can.

Pull your powerhouse into your spine so that you have a straight line from your left ankle to the top of your head. Find that place of balance.

ACTION

Inhale as you pull the powerhouse in toward your buttocks and sweep your leg gently forward. Keep it level, as if it were moving through a tunnel, until it is in front of your hip at a right angle to the body.

Exhale as you take your leg to the back. Keep it level.

Try this slowly 2 more times.

Now you can swing your leg front and back. Maintain the same control and keep your leg on an even level.

Repeat 5 times. Come back to center and repeat on the other side.

*T*HE MERMAID

> *This exercise is designed to give your baby more room by opening up your rib cage and stretching your waist.*

READY

Sit on your left hip with your knees bent and facing forward.

Place your right knee on top of the left and your right foot on top of the left.

Hold your right ankle with your right hand for balance.

Stretch your left arm straight up above your shoulder. There should be a straight line between your left hip and left hand.

Pull in your powerhouse and continue to lengthen along your entire left side.

ACTION

Let your left arm fall over your head and reach your body toward the right side. Feel the stretch in your left ribs.

Extend your left arm straight up again.

Pull down your lats. Keep your neck long.

Circle your left hand down to the mat, fingers pointing away from you.

Pull your powerhouse into your spine. Lengthen.

Stretch straight out to the left side as far as you can without coming off the mat.

Push up and come back to center. Repeat one more time.

Come up onto your knees and sit on your right hip.

Repeat on the other side.

$\mathcal{C}$AN-CAN

This exercise is great for slimming and creating definition in your waistline. It is also good for lengthening your thighs and hamstrings and releasing or stretching the lower back muscles.

READY

Lean on your hands, with your torso inclined at a 45° angle.

Lengthen your legs, extending them straight out from your hips, and bend your knees in toward you.

Place your toes on the floor and bring your knees as close to you as you can, keeping your legs and ankles together.

ACTION

Let your legs fall to the right side in that position so you're mainly on your right hip.

Bring them back through center and let them fall to your left side.

Do this 2 more times.

Keep your thighs where they are, pull in your powerhouse, and straighten your legs.

Bend your knees back again without moving your thighs and roll on your buttocks to the other side.

Keep your thighs together as you extend your legs.

Now pick up the tempo, moving to the cadence of "God Bless America."

Repeat 5 times.

*L*EG PULL-DOWN

> *This exercise will further develop coordination and balance. As
> you lift your leg, you will be pushing your heel back; as your leg
> comes down, you will be coming up on the ball of your foot. This
> will stretch your Achilles tendon and your calf muscles.*

READY

Come to a push-up position, keeping
your legs together. Your hands should
be directly underneath your shoulders,
fingertips facing forward. Your body is
flat as a board. You are looking straight
down, and your neck is long. Your
powerhouse is pulled tight into
your spine.

ACTION

Push your right heel back as your leg
extends out from the hip.

Come back on the ball of your foot,
heel over toes, as you bring the leg
down.

Your torso remains fixed, and the
buttocks stay tight.

Repeat as you lift your right leg.

Repeat 3 times.

89

*L*EG PULL-UP

This is a great exercise for your abs as well as your triceps and will heighten your sense of balance.

You don't want your pelvis to sink as you raise your leg, and you don't want your hips to shift. You can keep your hips square by pulling in your powerhouse and squeezing your buttocks tight.

READY

Both hands should now be underneath your shoulders, fingers facing out.

Squeeze your buttocks in toward your powerhouse and lift them up as high as you can.

Pull in your powerhouse even more. Your body is again flat, as you are now in the opposite position of a push-up. Glue your legs together and rest on your heels.

ACTION

Inhale and raise your right leg upward and toward you. It doesn't have to be high. It's just for control and strength.

Pull the lats down. Your neck should be long and relaxed.

Exhale as you bring your leg down.

Lift your pelvis up higher as you come down, and don't let it fall.

Continue to breathe evenly as you lift your leg up and down.

Repeat 3 times on each side.

ℙush-ups

> *With this exercise you can clearly see the lineage of Eastern disciplines in Pilates's work. This particular exercise is based on yoga's Solar Salutation. As you become more advanced in this work, when you reach the point of doing the push-up, you can put one ankle behind the other and keep that back leg extended throughout the exercise.*

READY

Stand tall at the end of the mat.

ACTION

Let the weight of your head bring it toward the mat.

Let the weight of your head bring the rest of your body down, so you're curling down, vertebra by vertebra, keeping the rib cage pulled in.

If you can touch your toes, great.
If not, it's okay.

Walk your hands out on the mat.

Make an A with your body.

Use your powerhouse to guide the weight of your body toward your hands until your entire body is flat, in a push-up position.

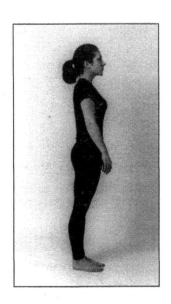

91

Inhale as you ease your body down toward the mat.

And exhale as you push up, keeping your entire body as straight as a board.

Do 5 push-ups.

Walk your hands back toward your feet, pushing your heels down into the mat.

Pull in your powerhouse and curl your pelvis underneath you as you stack one vertebra on top of the other.

Roll up slowly, letting your abs guide the movement.

Your head is the last part of your body to be stacked.

Take your arms up in the air and lift your chest to your chin.

Lift your upper body to your chest.

Don't arch your lower back, just your upper back.

Now let your arms fall to your sides and drop your head down.

Repeat 3 times.

ROWING SERIES

*R*OWING NUMBER 5

> *Designed to improve your posture, this exercise will create more room between your shoulder blades, make your chest feel open and lifted, and help release tension in your shoulders.*

READY

Sit cross-legged or whatever way is most comfortable for you.

Touch your forefingers and thumbs together to form a diamond shape with your hands.

Bend your elbows and place your diamond shape at the nape of your neck.

Keeping your shoulders relaxed, lean forward at a slight angle.

ACTION

Exhale.

93

Let your hands graze along the back of your head as you stretch your arms up parallel to the line of your straight back.

Inhale as you bend your elbows back to the starting position.

Repeat 5 times.

ℛOWING NUMBER 6

This exercise is excellent for the muscle tone in your upper arms and will improve your posture as well. If you choose, you may use light dumbbells for this exercise. If you do not use weights, apply isometric principles to create resistance while performing this exercise: Pretend that you are moving your body through wet cement. The closer that cement is to drying, the more resistance there is to your movement.

READY

Sitting cross-legged, pretend there is a string attached to your top vertebra and let that string be pulled gently upward so you are sitting up even taller than before.

Gently pull your scapula down and allow yourself to become even taller.

ACTION

With your arms comfortably at your sides, bend your elbows slightly so that your arms have a subtle curve.

Inhale.

Without changing the shape of your arms, use either isometric resistance or dumbbells to bring your arms out in front of you as if you were hugging a fairly large tree trunk.

Exhale.

Use the same amount of resistance and bring your arms back to your sides.

Repeat 4 times.

Now reverse your breathing.

Exhale as you hug the tree.

Inhale as your arms come back to the starting position.

Repeat 4 more times.

ROWING NUMBER 3

> *This is a challenging component of the Rowing Series. It is an excellent exercise that will promote proper breathing, enhance your coordination, and improve your posture.*

READY

Sit up straight, your legs extended in front of you, and point your feet.

Squeeze your buttocks so you can sit up even taller.

With your palms facing the mat, bring your elbows behind you and keep your hands at chest level.

ACTION

Inhale as you press your arms up into a sleepwalking position.

Keeping your back strong, exhale and bring your hands down to your thighs.

Feel long throughout the length of your torso.

Lift your arms up as you exhale.

Press your arms open to your sides as you exhale and bring your arms tightly back to your sides, bending your elbows for position one.

Repeat 3–5 times.

ROWING NUMBER 4

Again, this is a challenging part of the Rowing Series. This exercise will promote a better sense of balance and enhance your flexibility.

READY

Sit up tall with your arms by your sides and your palms pressing down.

Your legs should be stretched out long in front of you, and your feet should be flexed.

ACTION

Round your back gently and drop your head.

Slide your hands along the floor toward your ankles or past your feet if they will go that far.

Roll through your spine and reach your arms forward until your spine becomes straight and your arms are extended straight out.

Press your arms open, as if you are pressing the air away from you.

Release your arms and back and return to the starting position.

Repeat 10 times.

$\mathcal{T}$OTAL BUTT WORKOUT

This is not a Pilates exercise but one of my own. This workout really firms up the behind and is a favorite among pregnant women in my studio.

READY

Lie on your back. Your feet should be against the wall. Your legs should be at a 45° angle.

Put a ball between your knees and squeeze for ten counts.

Squeeze again.

Tweeze your buttocks together.

Come back to neutral and scoot yourself forward. Your legs are now against the wall at a right angle.

Tweeze your ribs into your powerhouse.

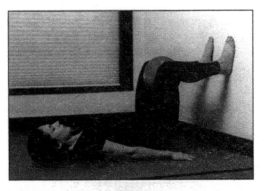

ACTION

Squeeze your buttocks and scoop up your hips. Imagine that your pelvis is like an ice-cream scoop. Keep your stomach in and scoop up.

Scoop your pelvis up toward your forehead.

Take your pelvis as high as you can without arching your back.

Release and come down vertebra by vertebra.

Repeat 20 times.

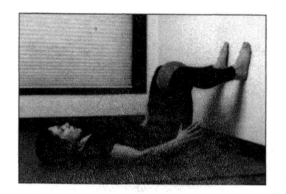

Scoop your pelvis toward your forehead and stay there.

Pulse upward.

Do you feel that in your butt?

Squeeze your buttocks as long as you can.

Repeat 50 times.

Come back down to neutral, vertebra by vertebra.

ℛolling
DOWN THE WALL

> *Here's a wonderful exercise to finish the session. This will really*
> *stretch out your lower back.*

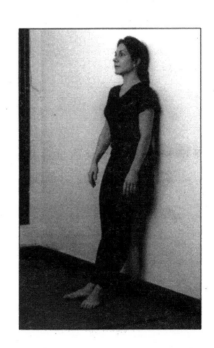

READY

Come to a standing position with your
back against the wall.

Your feet should be hip-width apart,
about 1 foot away from the wall.

Feel your entire spine against the wall.
Your shoulders should be open.

ACTION

Slowly let your head drop forward.

When your chin nears your chest, feel
the weight of your neck begin to lead
you down.

Pull in your ribs and continue to
stretch your neck and upper back.

Pull your powerhouse in toward
your spine.

103

Relax your entire upper body and let the weight of your head, neck, and upper body pull you over. You may even have to bend your knees slightly.

Scoop your pelvis underneath you.

Slide your pelvis up the wall as you straighten your legs.

Press your lower back against the wall.

Pull in your powerhouse as you roll up, vertebra by vertebra, until you are upright.

Repeat 3 times.

CHAPTER 7

SECOND-TRIMESTER WORKOUT

$\mathcal{T}$HE ONE HUNDRED

> *Through this exercise you are increasing your circulation and warming up your body with a combination of breath and movement. When you are finished, you should feel warmth around the area of your heart.*

PREP

Lie on your back. Feel your whole spine meet the floor. You should have the sensation that your spine is long and open. Your arms are at your sides and long against your body, and your palms are flat on the mat. Your knees are pointed to the ceiling, and your feet are flat on the mat.

READY

Use your powerhouse to bring your chin into your chest and continue that motion as you roll up.

Do *not* lift your upper body higher than the base of your shoulder blades.

Continue to press your lower back into the mat and maintain this necessary support for your spine.

ACTION

Pull your powerhouse tightly into your lower back.

Inhale slowly through your nose for five counts while pumping your arms up and down. Your arms should be rigid. Think of them as hammers pounding in nails.

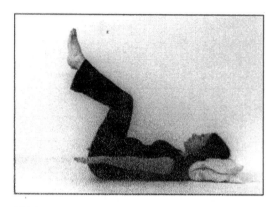

Exhale slowly through your nose for five counts, continuing to pump your arms up and down.

Use your powerhouse for support. Keep your arms straight. Keep only your arms and shoulders involved in the movement.

Repeat the cycle until you have counted up to 100.

Relax completely.

When you are ready, hug your knees into your chest to give your lower back a nice stretch. The bigger your growing tummy, the wider apart your knees will be.

$\mathcal{M}$ODIFIED ROLL-UPS

> *This exercise is a wonderful stretch for your lower back and will really put you in touch with your powerhouse. The powerhouse connects everything. As you do this exercise, try to feel that connection.*

READY

Sitting up tall, place your feet flat on the mat with your knees pointing toward the ceiling.

Place the palms of your hands underneath your thighs and point your elbows away from your body.

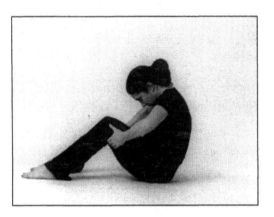

ACTION

Pull your navel into your spine. Let that contraction curve your lower back into the shape of a C. Roll back into that contraction until your arms are straight.

Pull in your powerhouse even further.

Now pull up with your arms and with your powerhouse, *not your back*.

Repeat 6–8 times.

As you feel your abs becoming stronger, do the same movement without your arms, relying only on your powerhouse.

$\int$INGLE LEG CIRCLES

In this exercise you are loosening your hips and stretching your hamstrings. Despite the name of the exercise, try to trace a rounded triangle, an oval, or a football shape using your leg. Keep the motion smooth. Use your powerhouse to support this motion and squeeze your buttocks for support.

READY

Lie flat on your back with your hands resting comfortably at your sides.

ACTION

Hug your right knee into your chest.

Keeping your leg aligned with your **hip**, relax your leg straight up.

Get as close to forming a right angle with your body as you comfortably can.

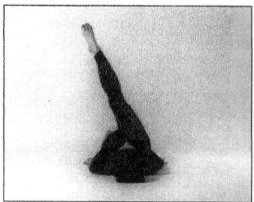

Without moving your hips, cross your leg in front of your body like a windshield wiper.

Once your leg is crossed, swing it down past your passive leg like a sickle by about 6 inches, then up toward the ceiling.

110

Stay within the frame of your body, keeping your leg aligned within your shoulders.

Repeat 5 circles in each direction.

Exhale slowly and change legs.

Now repeat 5 circles in each direction with this leg.

$\mathcal{S}$INGLE LEG STRETCH

> *This exercise is designed to work on your coordination, relax the hip flexors, and link breath to movement. As you concentrate on your powerhouse while you begin this movement, you will feel your abs strengthening. Keep your shoulders square. The only parts of your body that should move are your arms and legs.*

READY

Lie flat on your back.

Your legs should be extended directly out of your hips and relaxed flat against the mat. Your arms should rest down against your body, your palms flat on the mat.

ACTION

Inhale slowly and lift your chin toward your chest.

Use your powerhouse to raise your head and shoulders off the mat.

Simultaneously bend your right knee into your chest and place your right hand to the outside of your right ankle. Place your left hand atop the inside of your right knee.

Your shoulders are relaxed, your elbows are open.

Relax your ankle. Tug on your leg twice, breathing out as you go.

Now switch legs.

Repeat on the other side: Move your left hand to your left ankle, placing your right hand atop the inside of your left knee.

Keep your leg in alignment with your body.

Tug twice and switch.

Contract your powerhouse as you exhale and engage your stomach muscles at all times.

Repeat 5–10 times.

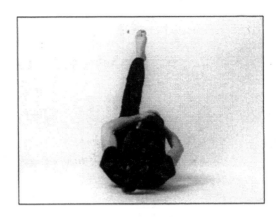

$\mathscr{D}$OUBLE LEG STRETCH

> *In this exercise you will be folding and unfolding your body, providing a nice stretch for your arms and legs. As your powerhouse pulls in, you fold. Imagine a comet hitting the earth, sucking everything into the hole its impact leaves on the surface. That's what your body is doing: The comet hits your powerhouse, and you fold in.*

READY

Glue your legs together.

Bring your knees in toward your chest and hug your ankles gently.

Use your powerhouse to lift your chin to your chest.

ACTION

As you inhale, lengthen your legs and lift them up toward the ceiling. Your torso should remain fixed.

Bring your arms up straight and long until they are even with your ears.

Your torso stays flat on the floor. It is fixed and does not move.

114

As you exhale, sweep your arms around by your sides.

Using your powerhouse, slowly draw your legs toward your abdomen and hug your ankles or shins.

Hold.

Using your powerhouse, stretch your limbs away from your torso then pull them back in.

Reach. Fold. Hug.

Repeat 5–10 times.

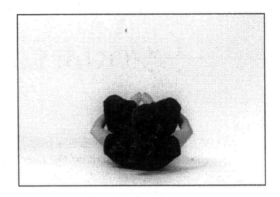

$\int$INGLE STRAIGHT LEG

> *This exercise is designed to increase flexibility in your legs, especially in your hamstrings, and to strengthen your abs. It is important to keep your lower back in contact with the mat.*

READY

From the Double Leg Stretch, bring your right leg straight up until it is perpendicular to the mat.

Extend your left leg straight out like an arrow coming out of your hip socket, until it is at either a 45° or 90° angle (whichever is more comfortable for you).

ACTION

Inhale as you reach your arms up and place your hands around your ankle if you can. If you can't, place them around your calf or your knee or the back of your thigh.

Lift your head, chin toward your chest, bringing your shoulders off the mat.

Keep those shoulders pressing down.

Exhale as you stretch your right leg further by tugging it toward you twice—one, two.

Pull in your powerhouse and switch legs in a scissorslike motion, bringing your left leg up toward your body.

Try not to move your torso.

Exhale as you pulse your left leg twice.

Let's add some tempo to the movement. Make it vigorous.

Inhale every 2 sets and exhale every 2 sets.

Repeat at least 10 times.

116

$\mathcal{S}$PINE STRETCH FORWARD

This exercise provides a good stretch for the entire back and will improve your posture. You can really lengthen your spine and create some space between the vertebrae with this exercise to make some more room inside for your baby.

READY

Sit up. Open your legs a bit wider than your shoulders. Push your heels away from you (i.e., flex your feet). Extend your arms forward as if you are sleepwalking. Use your powerhouse to lengthen your spine.

ACTION

As you exhale, pull your powerhouse into your spine. Make a C with your spine.

Lower your head and reach your arms forward.

Maintain the C curve, as if you are rounding over a beach ball.

Inhale.

Try not to roll back onto your seat.

Inhale as you roll back up and sit up tall.

Repeat 3 times.

When you finish reach toward your toes to get a nice stretch.

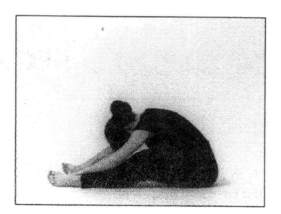

*N*ECK ROLL

Sit cross-legged, your back straight and your neck long.

Look slowly to your right.

Come back to center.

Look slowly to your left.

Repeat.

Tilt your head toward your right shoulder and circle your head around, the crown of your head leading the way. If you have trouble keeping your shoulders down, sit on your hands.

Reverse the circle.

Repeat twice.

119

$\int$AW

> *This exercise will promote proper breathing and is fantastic for wringing out the lungs. It also provides a deep stretch for your hamstrings and your entire side from your waist up. Keep your buttocks planted firmly and equally on the mat to maximize this stretch.*

READY

Lift up from your powerhouse and sit up tall. Your legs should be long against the mat, shoulder-width apart, with your kneecaps facing the ceiling.

Extend your arms out to the sides like airplane wings, keeping them in your peripheral sight. Use your powerhouse to support your lower back.

ACTION

Exhale as you glue your butt to the floor and use your powerhouse to twist slowly to the right. Twist from your waist, not from your hips.

Reach your left pinky toward your right little toe (your right arm will drop when it gets behind you).

Stretch your body forward over your right knee. Relax your neck and keep your opposite hip down.

Exhale slowly, getting out all the air in your lungs as you perform 3 sawlike motions.

Saw that little toe off. Stretch from your waist and finish exhaling.

Inhale.

Roll up and return to center.

Repeat on your left side.

Repeat 4 times.

$\int$IDE KICK SERIES

This exercise promotes muscular control and balance. The only portion of your body that should move throughout this exercise series is from your hips down. You should use the powerhouse to hold your torso still and fixed. In this series you will be lying on your side; body positioning is a key element of executing these exercises correctly. Your upper hip must stay directly on top of the other hip. It should not become displaced because of the movement. The torso should remain straight, long, and strong. This is a great exercise for the buttocks and thighs.

READY

Lie on your right side with your bottom arm extended straight up from your shoulder.

Your elbow is bent, your hand supporting your lifted head (use a pillow if this becomes uncomfortable).

Place your top arm in front of you with your hand flat on the mat for support.

Your shoulders should be down. Your legs should extend straight down from your hips, which should be stacked on top of one another. Your powerhouse is pulled in, and your lower back is long.

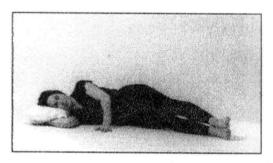

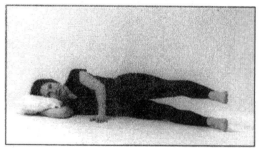

Bring both legs, glued together, up and forward about 8–12 inches, so your body forms an angle: From the waist up, you're perfectly straight. From the hips down, you're at an angle.

ACTION

Lift your top leg so it is even with your top hip. Your ankle should be relaxed.

Bring your leg forward as far as you comfortably can and pulse twice—one, two.

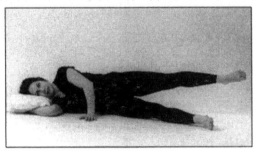

Think of your leg as an arrow coming out of your hip socket.

Keeping your torso fixed, bring your top leg down past your bottom leg and pulse twice to the back—one, two. Your powerhouse moves your leg.

Repeat 10 times.

$\mathscr{B}$ICYCLE FRONT/BACK

READY

Remain on your side with your head propped up by your arm.

Bring your top leg straight out in front of you so your foot is adjacent to your belly button and bend your knee without moving your thigh, keeping your knee hip-level.

ACTION

Take your heel to your buttocks, shifting that shape to the back, and then stretch your leg.

Bring your leg straight front.

Repeat 3 times.

Now reverse the direction for 3 more.

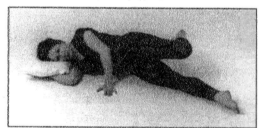

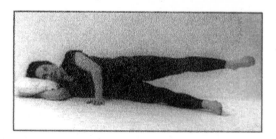

$\mathcal{L}$EG LIFTS

READY

Remain lying on your side with your head propped up.

Your legs should be extended straight down from your hips.

Rotate your top leg so your kneecap is facing the ceiling. One hip is on top of the other.

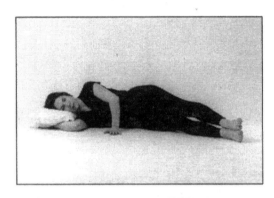

ACTION

Lift your top leg up and bring it straight down. Go only as far as your flexibility will allow. Don't force anything. Try not to let your upper hip roll back; keep it right in alignment with your lower hip.

Up and slowly down. And up and slowly down. It's a controlled kick.

Again, your torso stays still, and your stomach is pulled in. Don't forget to breathe.

Ankles are relaxed.

Repeat 10 times.

$\int$MALL LEG CIRCLES

READY

End the last exercise with one leg on top of the other. Think of your leg as an arrow coming out of your hip socket.

ACTION

Moving from the hip, draw a cantaloupe-sized circle with your leg. Try not to make a circle from your knee or ankle.

And reverse. That's it.

Keep your knees straight, use your powerhouse for support, and don't forget to breathe.

Repeat 10 times.

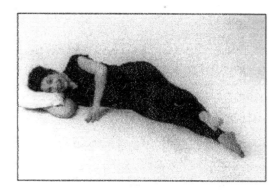

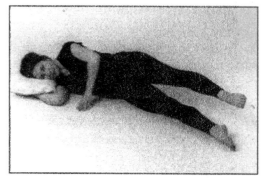

$\mathscr{L}$ARGE CIRCLES

READY

Keeping your torso still, reach forward
with your top leg.

ACTION

Draw a big circle with your toes.
Completely isolate your top leg,
guiding it with your hip by using your
powerhouse. Keep your hips and lower
leg still. Pull in that powerhouse. Don't
allow your torso to move back and
forth at all. If you're more advanced on
these, you can pick up the hand that's
on the floor and put it behind the other
ear: Then you really have to use your
abs for control.

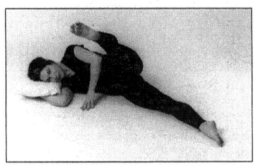

Reverse and repeat 5 times.

$\mathcal{H}$OT POTATO

READY

Remaining in the pike position, bring your top leg down.

ACTION

Lift your top leg, bring it about 6 inches in front of your bottom leg and tap it on the floor 3 times.

Making a half circle, move your top leg 6 inches in back of your bottom leg and tap it on the floor 3 times.

Add some more dynamics. Move your leg to the tempo of "God Bless America." Really move it—show why this is called "Hot Potato."

Repeat 5 times on each side.

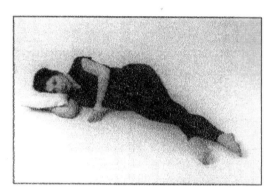

$\mathcal{S}$CISSORS

READY

You are still lying on your side with your head propped up on your hand.

Lift both legs about 6 inches above the mat, or as far as you comfortably can.

Don't roll your hips to the back; stack your legs on top of one another.

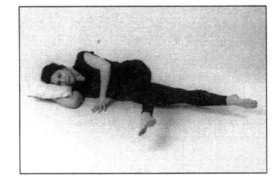

ACTION

One leg moves to the front as the other moves to the back.

Now switch, just like a pair of scissors. The movement is fluid and balanced.

Pick up the tempo. Big movement.

Give yourself some space between the ankles. That's it.

Your powerhouse is pushing in toward your spine.

Repeat 10 times.

NOW GO BACK TO PAGE 122, ROLL ONTO YOUR OTHER SIDE, AND COMPLETE THIS SERIES FOR THE OTHER LEG.

$\mathcal{L}$EG LIFTS

> *This series of four positions is not from traditional Pilates exercises but are of my own design. I find these leg lifts a fantastic continuation of the Side Kick Series, and a way to work the thighs even more. For best results, pretend your legs are moving through wet cement. The closer the cement is to drying, the more resistance there will be to your movements.*

READY

After the Scissors, bring your knees up, one leg directly on top of the other.

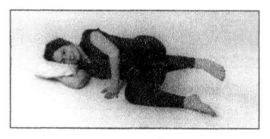

ACTION

Lift your top leg no higher than your hip. Release that leg down slowly into your starting position.

Repeat 20 times.

Turn your knee down so it is touching the opposite knee. Lift your leg. Slowly bring it back into your starting position.

Repeat 20 times.

Bend your knees. Bring your feet together. Open and close your legs like a clam.

Repeat 20 times.

Draw a circle with your knee—forward, up, down, together.

Repeat 20 times.

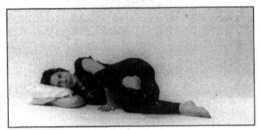

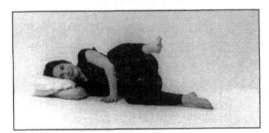

Turn over and repeat this exercise for your other leg.

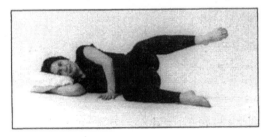

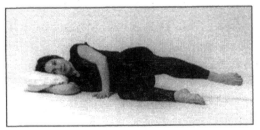

$\mathcal{T}$HE ASTRONAUT

The starting position for this exercise is similar to the Modified Roll-Up starting position. This exercise will help you strengthen various muscles that are used during delivery. If you feel cramping or pulling at any time, stop the exercise immediately.

READY

Start in a sitting position with the bottoms of your feet flat against the floor and your hands underneath the backs of your thighs.

Round your back and tighten your buttocks for additional support.

ACTION

Slowly release your arms forward and hold for a count of five.

Place your hands back under your thighs and rest for five counts.

Release your arms back into the starting position.

Repeat 2 more times.

132

$\mathcal{T}$HE MERMAID

This exercise is designed to open up your rib cage and stretch your entire torso. Not only will this exercise allow you to breathe more deeply, but it will give your baby more room inside of you. As your pregnancy progresses, you will have to open your knees a bit wider. Never hesitate to make the necessary adjustments.

READY

Sit on your left hip with your knees bent and facing forward.

Place your right knee on top of the left and your right foot on top of the left.

Hold your right ankle with your right hand for balance.

Stretch your left arm straight up above your shoulder. There should be a straight line between your left hip and left hand.

Pull in your powerhouse and continue to lengthen along your entire left side.

ACTION

Let your left arm fall over your head and reach your body toward the right side. Feel the stretch in your left ribs.

Extend your left arm straight up again.

Pull down your lats. Keep your neck long.

Circle your left hand down to the mat, fingers pointing away from you.

Pull your powerhouse into your spine. Lengthen.

Stretch straight out to the left side as far as you can without coming off the mat.

Push up and come back to center. Repeat one more time.

Come up onto your knees and sit on your right hip.

Repeat on the other side.

Repeat 3 more times.

$\int$PINE TWIST

> *The purpose of this exercise is to loosen up your spine and increase the flexibility in your hips and waist. What you are really doing is isolating your waist. To get the most out of this exercise, initiate the movement of twisting only from your waist. Think of your waist like a lid on a jar. If you were twisting the top off a jar, you would not want the bottom to move.*

READY

You are sitting tall with your legs extended straight out from the hips and your arms in the airplane wing position. All body parts are extended up and out, and your torso is high.

Pull down your lats. Your shoulders should be relaxed, your neck long.

ACTION

As you exhale, slowly twist from your waist to your right.

Look at your right hand as your left comes forward.

Ideally, when you have completed the twist, both hands will be in a straight line. Go as far as you comfortably can.

As you inhale, slowly come back to center.

Exhale as you twist to the left.

Switch and repeat.

Repeat 3 times.

$\mathcal{C}$ORKSCREW

> *This exercise will strengthen the muscles in your back and help you improve your balance.*

READY

Roll down to the mat vertebra by vertebra until you are lying flat on your back.

Your arms are straight down by your sides, your palms flat against the mat.

Lift your legs toward the ceiling, with the small of your back pressed against the mat.

ACTION

Glue your legs together.

Initiating from your powerhouse, move your legs to your left in a counterclockwise motion and with your toes outline a circle the size of a large pizza.

Inhale at 12:00. Exhale at 6:00.

Now reverse the circle.

Repeat 3 times.

CAN-CAN

> *This exercise is great for lengthening your thighs and hamstrings
> and releasing or stretching the lower back muscles.*

READY

You are seated in a reclining position.
You are leaning back on your hands.
Your back is straight and at a 45° angle.

Lengthen your legs, extending them
straight out from your hips, and bend
your knees in toward you.

Place your toes on the floor and bring
your knees as close to you as you can,
keeping your legs and ankles together.

ACTION

Let your legs fall to the right side in
that position so you're mainly on your
right hip.

Bring them back through center and let
them fall to your left side.

Repeat 2 times.

Keep your thighs where they are, pull in your powerhouse, and straighten your legs.

Bend your knees back again without moving your thighs and roll on your buttocks to the other side.

Keep your thighs together as you extend your legs.

Now pick up the tempo, if you can.

Repeat 3 times.

CHEST EXPANSION

READY

Kneel on the mat. Your legs are hip-width apart. Your arms extend straight out in a sleepwalking position. Pull in from your powerhouse to lengthen through your spine.

ACTION

Push your arms straight back as if you are pushing wet cement past your buttocks.

Push your arms back as far as they will go so you are open across your chest. Hold that position.

Keep your shoulders down.
Look to the right.

Come back to center.

Look to the left.

Come back to center.

Release your arms down to your sides.

Repeat 5–10 times.

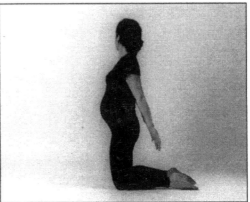

$\mathcal{T}$OTAL BUTT WORKOUT

[*This is not a Pilates exercise but one of my own. This is an excellent exercise to firm up the buttocks and thighs.*]

READY

Lie on your back. Your feet are against the wall. Your legs are at a 45° angle.

Put a ball between your knees and squeeze for ten counts.

Squeeze again.

Tweeze your buttocks together.

Come back to neutral. Scoot yourself forward. Your legs are now against the wall at a right angle.

Tweeze your ribs into your powerhouse.

ACTION

Squeeze your buttocks and scoop up your hips. Your pelvis is like an ice-cream scoop. Keep your stomach in and scoop up.

Scoop your pelvis up toward your forehead. Take your pelvis as high as you can without arching your back.

Release and come down vertebra by vertebra.

Repeat 20 times.

Scoop your pelvis toward your forehead and stay there.

Pulse upward.

Squeeze your buttocks as long as you can.

Repeat 50 times.

Come back down to neutral, vertebra by vertebra.

ROWING SERIES

ℛOWING NUMBER 5

This exercise will create more room between your shoulder blades, make your chest feel open and lifted, and help release the tension in your shoulders.

READY

Sit cross-legged or whatever way is most comfortable for you.

Touch your forefingers and thumbs together to formed a diamond shape with your hands.

Bend your elbows and place your diamond shape at the nape of your neck.

Keeping your shoulders relaxed, lean forward at a slight angle.

ACTION

Exhale.

Let your hands graze along the back of your head as you stretch your arms up parallel to the line of your straight back.

Inhale as you bend your elbows back to the starting position.

Repeat 5 times.

144

ROWING NUMBER 6

This exercise is excellent for the muscle tone in your upper arms and will improve your posture as well. If you choose, you may use light dumbbells (1–2 lbs.) for this exercise. If you do not use weights, apply isometric principles to create resistance while performing this exercise: Pretend that you are moving your body through wet cement. The closer that cement is to drying, the more resistance there is to your movement.

READY

Sitting cross-legged, pretend there is a string attached to your top vertebra and let that string be pulled gently upward so you are sitting up even taller than before.

Gently pull your scapula down and allow yourself to become even taller.

ACTION

With your arms comfortably at your sides, bend your elbows slightly so that your arms have a subtle curve.

Inhale.

Without changing the shape of your arms, use either isometric resistance or dumbbells to bring your arms out in front of you as if you were hugging a fairly large tree trunk.

Exhale.

Use the same amount of resistance and bring your arms back to your sides.

Repeat 4 times.

Now reverse your breathing.

Exhale as you hug the tree.

Inhale as your arms come back to the starting position.

Repeat 4 times.

ℛOWING NUMBER 3

> *This is a challenging component of the Rowing Series. It is an excellent exercise that will promote proper breathing, enhance your coordination, and improve your posture.*

READY

Sit up straight, your legs extended in front of you, and point your feet.

Squeeze your buttocks so you can sit up even taller.

With your palms facing the mat, bring your elbows behind you, keeping your hands at chest level.

ACTION

Inhale as you press your arms up into a sleepwalking position.

Keeping your back strong, exhale and bring your hands down to your thighs.

Feel long throughout the length of your torso.

Lift your arms up as you inhale.

Press your arms open to your sides as you exhale and bring your arms tightly back to your sides, bending your elbows for position one.

Repeat 3–5 times.

ROWING NUMBER 4

Again, this is a challenging part of the Rowing Series. This exercise will promote a better sense of balance and enhance your flexibility.

READY

Sit up tall with your arms by your sides and your palms pressing down.

Your legs are stretched out long in front of you, and your feet are flexed.

ACTION

Round your back gently and drop your head.

Slide your hands along the floor toward your ankles or past your feet if they will go that far.

Roll through your spine and reach your arms forward until your spine becomes straight and your arms are extended straight out.

Press your arms open, as if you are pressing the air away from you.

Release your arms and back and return to the starting position.

Repeat 10 times.

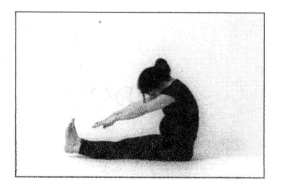

ROLLING
DOWN THE WALL

This will really stretch out your lower back. The trick is to completely relax your body. If you feel pressure in your tummy, do not continue the exercise.

READY

Come to a standing position with your back against the wall.

Your feet are hip-width apart, about 1 foot away from the wall.

Feel your entire spine against the wall. Your shoulders are open.

ACTION

Slowly let your head drop forward.

When your chin nears your chest, feel the weight of your neck begin to lead you down.

Pull in your ribs and continue to stretch your neck and upper back.

151

Pull your powerhouse in toward your spine.

Relax your entire upper body and let the weight of your head, neck, and upper body pull you over. You may even have to bend your knees slightly.

Scoop your pelvis underneath you.

Slide your pelvis up the wall as you straighten your legs.

Press your lower back against the wall.

Pull your powerhouse in as you roll up, vertebra by vertebra, until you are upright.

Repeat 3 times.

LITTLE PIECE OF HEAVEN

> *My mentor, Romana, named this exercise. We have been arching and working the lower back, and now it's time to give that area a little reward. If your knees hurt when you are rounded over, simply place a pillow between your buttocks and heels.*

READY

Position yourself on all fours.

ACTION

Use your hands and arms to push yourself back onto your heels until you are kneeling with your back rounded over. Your head is focused toward the mat. Your arms are extended long in front of you.

Push your hips to your heels for a deep lower back stretch.

Doesn't this feel great? Breathe slowly and deeply. Rest your back.

$\mathcal{L}$EGS
AGAINST THE WALL

This exercise is a fantastic way to rest your legs and back and a great way to end your session. Make sure your hips are not too close to the wall. Depending on how flexible you are in your back and hamstrings, you can determine a comfortable distance. Don't push it. The trick is to make sure your buttocks remain solidly on the mat.

Breathe deeply and evenly. Just relax, but do not exceed 5 minutes in this position.

CHAPTER 8

THIRD-TRIMESTER
WORKOUT

MODIFIED ONE HUNDRED

This exercise, designed to increase and maximize circulation, is a modified version of the one you did in your first and second trimesters. Through this exercise you are warming up the body with breath and movement. When you are finished, you should feel warmth around the heart area. If you become too uncomfortable on your back, kneel with your knees hip-width apart and keep the arm movements exactly the same.

PREP

Lie on your back. Feel your whole spine meet the floor. The spine is long and open. Your arms are long against your body, palms face down, flat on the mat. Your knees are pointed to the ceiling and your feet flat on the mat.

READY

If it is comfortable, use your powerhouse to bring your chin into your chest.

Do *not* lift your upper body higher than the base of your shoulder blades.

If this is too uncomfortable, rest your head on a pillow.

If even that is uncomfortable, kneel with your knees hip-width apart.

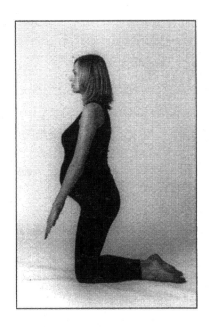

ACTION

Pull your powerhouse tightly into your lower back.

Inhale slowly through your nose for five counts while pumping your arms up and down.

Your arms should be rigid. Think of them as hammers pounding in nails.

Exhale slowly through the nose for five counts, continuing to pump your arms up and down.

Push all that air out. Keep your arms straight. Keep just your arms and shoulders involved in the movement.

Repeat the cycle until you have counted up to 100.

Relax completely.

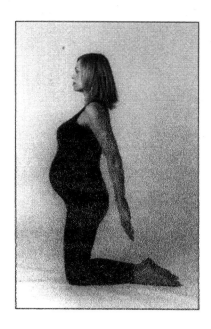

MODIFIED ROLL-UPS

This exercise will really put you in touch with your powerhouse and provide a great stretch for your lower back.

READY

Sitting up tall, place your feet flat on the mat with your knees pointing toward the ceiling.

Place the palms of your hands underneath your thighs and point your elbows away from your body.

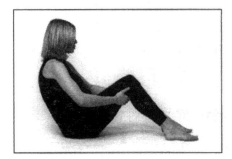

ACTION

Pull your navel into your spine. Let that contraction curve your lower back into the shape of a C. Roll back into that contraction until your arms are straight.

Now pull with your arms and with your powerhouse, *not your back*.

Repeat 6–8 times.

As you feel your abs becoming stronger, do the same movement without your arms, relying only on your powerhouse.

159

$\mathcal{S}$INGLE LEG CIRCLES

> *In this exercise you are loosening your hips and stretching your hamstrings. Despite the name of the exercise, try to trace a rounded triangle, an oval, or a football shape using your leg. Keep the motion smooth. Use your powerhouse to support this motion and squeeze your buttocks for support. Even if your oval is the size of a goose egg, you are doing just fine. Always do what you can and modify the exercise so you can continue the routine.*

READY

Lie flat on your back with your hands resting comfortably at your sides.

ACTION

Hug your right knee into your chest.

Keeping your leg aligned with your hip, relax your leg straight up. Bend your bottom leg slightly to become more comfortable.

Get as close as you comfortably can to forming a right angle with your body.

Without moving your hips, cross your leg in front of your body like a windshield wiper.

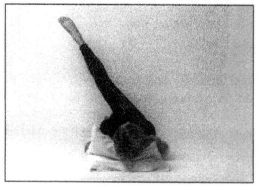

160

Once your leg is crossed, swing it down past your passive leg like a sickle by about 6 inches, then up toward the ceiling.

Stay within the frame of your body, keeping your leg aligned within your shoulders.

Cross your leg in front of your face.

Repeat this motion 3 times.

Exhale slowly and change legs.

Pull your left leg into your chest and extend your right leg out.

Do 5–10 sets.

$\int$PINE STRETCH FORWARD

This exercise provides a nice stretch for your entire back. You can really create some space between the vertebrae and create a tactile sensation of lengthening the spine. All of this will provide your baby more with room. They key to performing this exercise correctly is to gently contract the powerhouse into the spine and intensify that contraction throughout the exercise. In your third trimester, you do not want to push this contraction as far as you possibly can. Do only what feels good.

READY

Sit up. Open your legs a bit wider than your hips. Push your heels away from you (i.e., flex your feet). Extend your arms forward as if you are sleepwalking. Use your powerhouse to lengthen your spine.

ACTION

As you exhale, pull your powerhouse into your spine.

Continue the contraction, making a curve with your spine.

Maintain the C curve, and continue to exhale.

Reach forward with your arms.

Reach forward with the upper portion of your torso while maintaining your contraction and keeping your hipbones over your sit bones. Your buttocks should feel as if they are glued to the floor.

Inhale as you roll back up.

Repeat 3 times.

$\int$AW

> *This exercise will stretch your hamstrings and your whole side from your waist up. Again, as you lengthen the entire torso, you will be providing more room for the baby inside of you. Keep your buttocks equally and firmly planted on the mat to maximize this stretch. You should be particularly gentle when you twist during your third trimester.*

READY

Lift up from your powerhouse and sit up tall. Your legs should be long against the mat, shoulder-width apart, with your kneecaps facing the ceiling.

Extend your arms out to the sides like airplane wings, keeping them in your peripheral sight.

Gently pull your powerhouse into your lower back, with your shoulders pressing down toward your lats.

ACTION

Exhale as you glue your butt to the floor and use your powerhouse to twist slowly to the right. Twist from your waist, not from your hips.

Reach your left pinky toward your right little toe.

Stretch your body forward over your right knee. Relax your neck and keep your opposite hip down.

Exhale slowly as you perform 3 sawlike movements. Saw that little toe off.

Stretch from your waist.

Complete the exhalation from your powerhouse and then roll up and return to center.

Repeat on your left side.

Repeat 4 times.

$\mathcal{M}$ODIFIED NECK ROLL

Sit cross-legged or however you feel most comfortable.

Rest your hands on top of your thighs. Inhale and tilt your right ear toward your right shoulder.

In a half circle, sweep your head to your left, the crown of your head leading the way, until your left ear is facing your left shoulder.

Reverse the circle.

Repeat twice.

166

$\mathcal{J}$IDE KICK SERIES

> *The only portion of your body that should move throughout this exercise series is from your hips down. You should use the powerhouse to hold your torso still and fixed. You will be lying on your side; body positioning is a key element of executing the exercises in this series correctly. Your upper hip must stay directly on top of the other hip. It should not become displaced because of the movement. The torso should remain straight, long, and strong. This is a great exercise for the buttocks and thighs and also promotes control and balance.*

READY

Lie on your right side. Your bottom arm should be extended straight up from your shoulder.

Your elbow is bent, your hand supporting your lifted head.

Place your top arm in front of you with your hand flat on the mat for support.

Shoulders are down. Your legs extend straight down from your hips, which are stacked on top of one another. Your powerhouse is pulled in, and your lower back is long.

167

Bring both legs, glued together, up and forward about 8–12 inches so your body forms an angle, in what's known as a pike position.

ACTION

Lift your top leg so it is no higher than your top hip.

Bring your leg forward as far as you comfortably can and pulse twice—one, two.

Think of your leg as an arrow coming out of your hip socket.

Now keeping your torso fixed, bring your top leg down past your bottom leg and pulse twice to the back—one, two. Your powerhouse moves your leg.

Repeat 10 times.

$\mathcal{B}$ICYCLE FRONT/BACK

READY

Remain on your side with your head propped up by your arm.

Bring your top leg straight out in front of you so your foot is adjacent to your belly button, and bend your knee without moving your thigh, keeping your knee hip-level.

ACTION

Take your heel to your buttocks, shifting that shape to the back, and then stretch your leg.

Bring your leg straight front.

Repeat 3 times.

Now reverse the direction for 3 more.

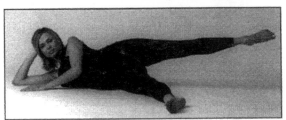

$\mathscr{L}$EG LIFTS

READY

Remain lying on your side with your head propped up.

Your legs are extended straight down from your hips in the pike position.

Rotate your top leg so the kneecap is facing the ceiling. One hip is on top of the other.

ACTION

Lift your top leg up and bring it straight down. Go only as far as your flexibility will allow. Don't force anything. Try not to let your upper hip roll back; keep it right in alignment with your lower hip.

Up and slowly down. And up and slowly down. It's a controlled kick.

And up and slowly down.

Again, your torso stays still, and your stomach is pulled in. Don't forget to breathe.

Ankles are relaxed.

Repeat 10 times.

170

$\int$MALL LEG CIRCLES

READY

End the last exercise with one leg on top of the other. Think of your leg as an arrow coming out of your hip socket.

ACTION

Moving from the hip, draw a cantaloupe-sized circle with the leg. Try not to make a circle from your knee or ankle.

And reverse. That's it.

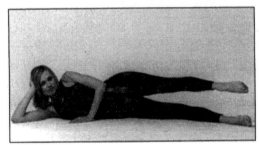

Keep your knees straight, stomach in, and remember to breathe.

Repeat 10 times.

ℒARGE CIRCLES

READY

Keeping your torso still, reach forward with your top leg.

ACTION

Draw a big circle with your toes. Completely isolate your top leg, guiding it with your hip by using your powerhouse. Keep your hips and lower leg still. Pull in that powerhouse. Don't let your torso move back and forth at all. If you're more advanced on these, you can pick up the hand that's on the floor and put it behind the other ear: Then you really have to use your abs for control.

5 circles each direction.

172

*H*OT POTATO

READY

Release your top leg down.

ACTION

Lift your top leg, bring it about 6 inches in front of your bottom leg and tap it on the floor 3 times.

Making a half circle, move your top leg 6 inches in back of your bottom leg and tap it on the floor 3 times.

Add some more dynamics. Move your leg to the tempo of "God Bless America."

Repeat 8 times on each side.

$\mathcal{I}$NNER THIGHS

READY

With your body in the pike position, draw your top leg up toward your opposite knee or thigh. Take hold of your ankle.

ACTION

Lift your bottom leg straight up until it is a few inches off the mat.

Raise and lower that leg 20 times, with the accent on the up beat.

Raise that leg another 2 inches and perform another set of 20.

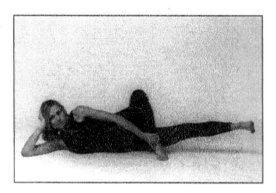

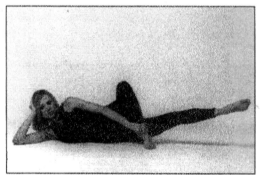

$\mathcal{J}$CISSORS

READY

You are still lying on your side with your head propped up on your hand.

Lift both legs about 6 inches above the mat, or as far as you comfortably can.

Don't roll your hips to the back; stack your legs on top of one another, using your hand in front for support.

ACTION

One leg moves to the front as the other moves to the back.

Now switch, just like a pair of scissors. The movement is fluid and balanced.

Pick up the tempo. Big movement.

Give yourself some space between the ankles.

Your powerhouse is pushing in toward your spine.

Repeat 10 times.

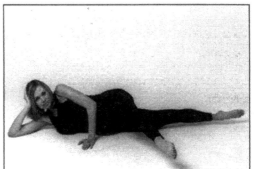

NOW GO BACK TO PAGE 167, ROLL ONTO YOUR OTHER SIDE, AND COMPLETE THIS SERIES FOR THE OTHER LEG.

*L*EG LIFTS

> *This series of four positions is not from traditional Pilates exercises but is of my own design. I find these leg lifts a fantastic continuation of the Side Kick Series, and a way to work the thighs even more. For best results, pretend your legs are moving through wet cement. The closer the cement is to drying, the more resistance your movements will encounter.*

READY

After the Scissors, bring your knees up, one leg directly on top of the other.

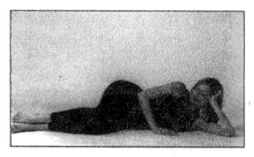

ACTION

Lift your top leg no higher than your hip. Release that leg down slowly into your starting position.

Repeat 20 times.

Turn your knee down so it is touching the opposite knee. Lift your leg. Slowly bring it back into your starting position.

Repeat 20 times.

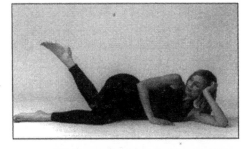

Bend your knees and bring your feet together. Open and close your legs like a clam.

Repeat 20 times.

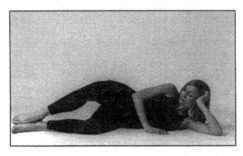

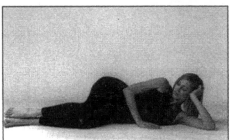

Draw a circle with your knee—forward, up, down, together.

Repeat 20 times.

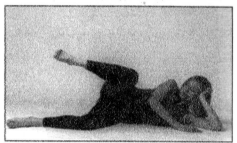

Roll over and repeat the entire exercise for your other leg.

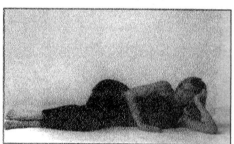

$\int$PINE TWIST

> *The purpose of this exercise is to loosen up your spine and increase flexibility in your hips and waist. What you are really doing is isolating your waist. To get the most out of this exercise, initiate the movement of twisting only from your waist. You will be watching the hand that is moving. The motion is like sweeping back a circular shower curtain. Don't make the mistake of letting that moving hand initiate the motion. You don't want to force the sweeping movement, and you should twist only as far as you comfortably can.*

READY

You are sitting tall with your legs extended straight out from the hips and your arms in the sleepwalking position. Everything is reaching forward. Your torso is high.

Pull down your lats. Your shoulders are relaxed. Your neck is long.

ACTION

As you exhale, slowly twist from your waist to your right.

Look at your right hand and let the movement of your right arm take your torso with you. Your left hand remains forward.

Ideally, when you have completed the twist, both hands will be in a straight line. Go as far as you comfortably can.

As you inhale, slowly bring your right arm back to the sleepwalking position.

Exhale as you twist to the left.

Switch and repeat.

Repeat 3 times.

THE ASTRONAUT

The starting position for this exercise is similar to the Modified Roll-Up starting position. This exercise will help you strengthen various muscles that are used during delivery. If you feel cramping or pulling at any time, stop the exercise immediately.

READY

Start in a sitting position with the bottoms of your feet flat against the floor and your hands underneath the backs of your thighs.

Round your back and tighten your buttocks for additional support.

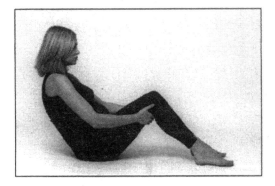

ACTION

Slowly release your arms forward and hold for a count of five.

Place your hands back under your thighs and rest for five counts.

Release your arms back into the starting position.

Repeat 2 more times.

181

$\mathcal{T}$HE MERMAID

This exercise is designed to open up your rib cage and stretch your waist.

TRANSITION

You are sitting on your left hip with your knees bent and facing forward (right knee on top of the left, right foot on top of the left).

READY

Hold your right ankle with your right hand for balance.

Stretch your left arm straight up above your shoulder. There should be a straight line between your left hip and left hand.

Pull in your powerhouse and continue to lengthen along your entire left side.

ACTION

Let your left arm fall over your head and reach your body toward the right side. Feel the stretch all along your left side as you exhale.

Extend your left arm straight up again.

Pull down your lats. Keep your neck long.

Circle your left hand down to the mat, fingers pointing away from you.

Pull your powerhouse into your spine. Lengthen.

Stretch straight out to the left side as far as you can without coming off the mat.

Push up and come back to center. Repeat one more time.

Come up onto your knees and sit on your right hip.

Repeat on the other side.

Repeat 2 more times.

CHEST EXPANSION

READY

Kneel on the mat with your legs hip-width apart. Your arms extend straight out in a sleepwalking position. Pull in from your powerhouse to lengthen through your spine.

ACTION

Push your arms straight back as if you are pushing wet cement past your buttocks; inhale.

Push your arms back as far as they will go so you are open across your chest. Hold that position and your breath.

Keep your shoulders down. Look to the right.

Come back to center.

Look to the left.

Come back to center.

Release your arms up into the sleepwalking position as you exhale.

Repeat 5–10 times.

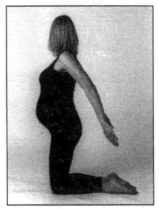

ℛOWING NUMBER 6

This exercise is excellent for the muscle tone in your upper arms and will improve your posture as well. If you choose, you may use one-pound dumbbells for this exercise. If you do not use weights, apply isometric principles to create resistance while performing this exercise: Pretend that you are moving your body through wet cement. The closer that cement is to drying, the more resistance there is to your movement.

READY

Sitting cross-legged, pretend there is a string attached to your top vertebra and let that string be pulled gently upward so you are sitting up even taller than before.

Gently pull your scapula down and allow yourself to become even taller.

ACTION

With your arms comfortably at your sides, bend your elbows slightly so that your arms have a subtle curve.

Inhale.

Without changing the shape of your arms, use either isometric resistance or dumbbells to bring your arms out in front of you as if you were hugging a fairly large tree trunk.

Exhale.

Use the same amount of resistance and bring your arms back to your sides.

Repeat 4 times.

Now reverse your breathing.

Exhale as you hug the tree.

Inhale as your arms come back to the starting position.

Repeat 4 more times.

$\mathcal{N}$ECK STRETCH

READY

Sit up straight with your legs crossed in front of you.

ACTION

Place the palm of your right hand on the mat with your fingers pointed toward you.

Now sit on your hand.

Extend your left arm straight up to the ceiling directly above your shoulder.

Curve your arm over your head and *gently* pull your head toward your left shoulder.

Feel the stretch along the right side of your neck.

Come back to center and repeat on the other side.

Sit on your left hand.

Turn your head slightly and relax your head toward your right shoulder, pointing your nose toward your armpit.

Bring your right hand over the top of your head and let it rest on the back of your head.

Let the weight of your right arm stretch your neck as your right elbow releases down toward the mat. Breathe into the stretch.

Pull into your powerhouse and deepen the stretch.

With your head at this 45° angle, release your arm and bring your head slowly back to center.

Repeat on the other side.

Repeat 3 times.

LITTLE PIECE OF HEAVEN

> *You can perform this exercise at any time during your workout. Whenever you feel your lower back becoming constricted or pinched, by all means do this exercise. As your pregnancy progresses, you will find that you can adjust this position and make it more comfortable by widening your knees. If your knees hurt when you are rounded over, simply place a pillow between your buttocks and heels. This is a fantastic exercise to rest your back muscles and open up your lower back.*

READY

Position yourself on all fours.

ACTION

Use your hands and arms to push yourself back onto your heels until you are kneeling with your back rounded over. Your head is focused toward the mat. Your arms are extended long in front of you.

Push your hips to your heels for a deep lower back stretch.

Doesn't this feel great? Breathe slowly and deeply. Rest your back.

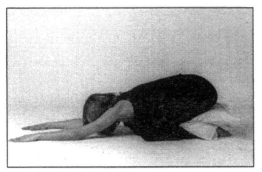

CHAPTER 9

AFTER DELIVERY— WHAT NEXT?

*A*FTER YOUR DELIVERY, you will want to become active as soon as you are able. If you did not have a C-section, an episiotomy, or an unusually large blood loss, you could theoretically perform the routine for the third trimester the day after your delivery. Consult with your doctor.

You will notice that you have excessive water weight. Throughout the birthing process all of the water surrounding your baby and all of the milk going into your breasts has mildly overwhelmed your body, and you just cannot urinate away all of the extra fluid in your system. By practicing even the simplest Pilates exercises, you will increase your circulation, and this should reduce swelling in your ankles or other joints.

When you and your doctor agree that it is time to begin exercising again, I suggest that whatever you do, you include Pilates in that regimen. Perhaps you could ease back into an active life-style by practicing the routine for the third trimester. Unless you suffered an illness or injury during your delivery, you should be doing the first-trimester workout within a couple of weeks. After that, I recommend picking up *The Pilates Powerhouse* and learning the complete Pilates mat routine. During your pregnancy you have used Pilates to supplement the exercise regimen prescribed by your doctor, but the Pilates mat routine is a total, stand-alone workout.

Pilates can indeed be all things to all people. Up to this point, you have been working to become extremely strong, especially within your powerhouse, and also to improve your control and coordination of movement. You could continue work with the mat routine and be perfectly satisfied that you are challenged, never becoming bored with the routine. But you may want to advance to a higher level in this work. If you want to build muscle, it is absolutely possible to do this by using the various Pilates machines. If you want to really sweat, a speedier workout on the machines would get the job done. Whatever your needs, Pilates can provide a solution. Each instructor has both a respect for the scientific tradition of Pilates and also her or his own orientation to fitness. Pilates is in a state of rapid evolution, and there are many qualified people branching off from or adding to this very rich and encompassing method of conditioning.

This chapter discusses some options as you begin to master this method of body conditioning. I discuss some equipment that was developed by Joseph Pilates and talk about looking for a studio to work on these machines or purchase them for home use. I bring up some questions that you should ask your trainer before you begin working out.

When you are performing mat work, you are working with the resistance and strength of your own body. It's just you and your body. When you do this work on equipment specifically designed for the movement, it accentuates all the resistance-oriented exercises that you're doing, making you work against even more resistance. Instead of simply imagining that you are moving through wet cement, as I often suggest, you are working with springs or pulleys that provide actual resistance. This resistance is non-weight-bearing, so you're not pumping or gasping for air, and as with the mat routine, you are limiting the possibility of injury. The equipment may allow you to take the mat work a step further and may even help you to develop musculature faster.

PILATES EQUIPMENT

On your first visit to a Pilates studio, you will be confronted with an array of machines that may be a little intimidating. Have no fear: You have been doing the same exercises on the mat. The only function these machines have is to create resistance, enabling you to have a deeper stretch. It may be helpful to introduce you to these machines so that if you do decide to try them, you will know their names and functions.

The first machine you would encounter at a Pilates studio would most probably be the Reformer. This is the main piece of equipment in a studio. It is the workhorse. Probably originally fashioned from a bed, it is rectangular and about 7 feet long, approximately the size of a full-sized mattress, and it stands about 6 inches off the floor. On top of the frame is a 4-foot-long padded board that you lie on top of. This board is on a carriage so that it can slide the entire length of the frame. The frame is capable of transforming itself with cables, springs, and pulleys to take many shapes and accommodate many body positions. With minor adjustment, most of the mat routine can be done on this machine.

Another machine is the Cadillac. This has about the same proportions as the Reformer, except that the bed is 4 feet off the ground, and it does not have a movable carriage. It is designed like a canopy bed and is close to 9 feet tall. An array of straps, springs, and pulleys can be attached to provide buoyancy and resistance for the legs. I believe that Pilates was inspired to build this by clientele that were hospitalized and in traction. This particular machine is my personal favorite, and I have found it very helpful in toning musculature.

Joseph Pilates was a circus performer, and many of his early devotees were also from the circus. The materials for his machinery had to be readily available and easy to transport, and it also had to be functional when not in use as training equipment. A perfect example of this can be found in another important piece of equipment, the Wunda Chair. When not put to use as an exercise device, the Wunda Chair could be placed at your kitchen table. But when it is turned on its side and the seat is folded back, it can be fitted with a vast array of springs, becoming one of the most advanced pieces of Pilates equipment. Almost all the exercises you have been practicing can be modified to work with the Wunda Chair.

Pilates studios usually also include two barrel-shaped devices used primarily for deep stretching. The Spine Corrector Barrel is padded and sits about 2 feet off the ground. This device is fantastic for people with scoliosis and osteoporosis. It is also a highly effective way to find the strength in your powerhouse and your stomach that would allow optimal support. The Spine Corrector Barrel provides the least diversity in terms of the number of exercises that it is intended for; when you are working with the diseases I just mentioned, however, this piece of equipment is irreplaceable. The High Barrel is actually a ladder with a padded barrel on top and resembles a curved vaulting horse. This apparatus is used for a very advanced series of exercises and for deep stretching.

Each one of these devices has many exercises specifically designed for the apparatus. Because you have become familiar with the principles of this method of body conditioning, the philosophy behind this equipment will not be foreign to you. What will be somewhat different will be working with a machine. The mat work that you are learning to master will help you to trust yourself a great deal and to trust in your body. This mastery is really a process of the mind and the body becoming one. When you work on these machines, you have to learn to become one with the device, to allow the straps, springs, and pulleys to act as extensions of your own limbs. This takes some getting used to, and you should have a professional trainer there to guide you.

HOW TO FIND A
PILATES STUDIO

I am amazed to see just how many Pilates studios are out there now. What was once a fairly obscure method of body conditioning is now becoming a force within the fitness community. No matter where you live, there should be someplace or someone available to train you.

The Appendix gives a complete list of certified Pilates instructors in the United States. If there is no studio or instructor in your area, call 1–800–4PILATE. This number will connect you with the Pilates Studio of New York, and they may be able to provide further assistance.

If you happen to find a teacher who is not certified through the Pilates Studio in New York, it's important that you ask some questions.

Just because she or he is not certified doesn't necessarily mean that she or he is a poor teacher, but you want to find out about a few qualifications. Where did the instructor study? What is her or his background— is it in physical fitness or dance? The more background people have that includes expertise in physical training, the more adept they usually are at passing on practical information during an actual workout. You'll want to make sure that the person has trained under someone, not just learned from a book or video. Find out all of a potential instructor's credentials. It doesn't hurt to ask. It is your body.

THE
PILATES STUDIO®
CERTIFYING CENTERS

© Copyright 2001 Pilates Inc.
The Pilates Studio® is a registered trademark of Pilates Inc.

FLORIDA

Fort Myers

The Pilates Studio® of Fort Myers
Melissa Derstine, Director and Instructor
11751 Cleveland Avenue, Suites 21 & 22
Ft. Myers, FL 33907
(941) 274–5711
Fax: (941) 274–6622

GEORGIA

Atlanta

The Pilates Studio® at the Atlanta Ballet
Denise Reeves, Director and Instructor
4279 Roswell Road, #208
Atlanta, GA 30342
(404) 459–9555
Fax: (404) 459–9455

ILLINOIS

Evanston

The Pilates Studio® of the Midwest
Fatima Bruhns, Director and Instructor
820 Davis Street, Suite 202
Evanston, IL 60201
(847) 492–0464
Fax: (847) 492–0210

NEW YORK CITY

West Side

The Pilates Studio®
Sean P. Gallagher, PT, Director
2121 Broadway, Suite 201 at 74th
New York, NY 10023
(212) 875–0189
Fax: (212) 769–2368
To purchase products: (888) 278–7227

East Side

Drago's Gym
Romana Kryzanowska,
      Sari Santo, Master Teachers
50 West 57th Street, 6th Floor
New York, NY 10019
(212) 757–0724

PENNSYLVANIA

Philadelphia

The Pilates Studio® at the P.A. Ballet
June Hines, Director and Instructor
1101 South Broad Street
Philadelphia, PA 19147
(215) 551–7000 x 1303
Fax: (215) 551–7224

Bryn Mawr

The Pilates Studio® of Bryn Mawr
Megan Egan, Director and Instructor
899 Penn Street
Bryn Mawr, PA 19010
(610) 581–0222
Fax: (610) 581–0223

WASHINGTON

Seattle

The Pilates Studio® of Seattle & Capitol Hill Physical Therapy
Lauren Stephen, Director and Instructor
Lori Coleman Brown, PT, Director
      and Instructor
413 Fairview Avenue North
Seattle, WA 98109
(206) 405–3560
Fax: (206) 405–3938

AUSTRALIA

Surry Hills

The New York Pilates Studio® of Australia
Cynthia Lochard, Director and Instructor
Roula Kantarzoglou, Edwina Ward, Instructors
Suite 12, Level 4/46–56
Holt Street
Surry Hills 2010
Australia
Tel/Fax: 011–612–9698–4689
www.pilatesm.com

BRAZIL

São Paulo

The Pilates Studio®
Inelia Garcia, Director and Instructor
Robero Souza Estevam, Cecilia Panelli Delgado, Instructors

R. Cincinato Braga, 520
Bela Vista–São Paulo
Brazil
Tel/Fax: 011–551–1284–8905
ineliagarcia@hotmail.com

NETHERLANDS

The Hague

The New York Pilates Studio® of the Netherlands
Marjorie Oron, Jane Poerwoatmodjo, Instructors
Keizerstraat 32
2584 BJ The Hague
Netherlands
011–31–703–508–684
Fax: 011–31–703–228285
Marjorie@pilates.nl

PILATES GUILD™
CERTIFIED INSTRUCTORS

ALABAMA

Gulf Shores

New Body
Misti McKee-Whaley, Instructor
112 Windmill Ridge Road
Gulf Shores, AL 36542
(334) 948–6036
Tilawoop@zebra.net

ALASKA

Fairbanks

Ann Turner, Instructor
3820 Ullrbahn Road
Fairbanks, AK 99709
(907) 479–2360
aturner@mosquitonet.com

ARIZONA

Phoenix

Fitness Solutions, Inc.
Lauren Tomasulo, Owner and Instructor
Garry Rogers, Laura Talla, Instructors
4515 North 16th Street, Suite 113
Phoenix, AZ 85016
(602) 631–9698

Center Fitness
Garry Rogers, Instructor
PO Box 16952
Phoenix, AZ 85011
(602) 843–4879
garryrinaz@aol.com

Pamela More, Instructor
Tel/Fax: (602) 569–1612

DBA Mind Over Matter
Pamela LaPierre, Instructor
5338 East Calle Redonda
Phoenix, AZ 85018
(602) 817–4402
Roobeenpac@aol.com

Tia Peterson, Instructor
(602) 224–5220
t1window@earthlink.net

Scottsdale

Pratibha Noggle, Instructor
raventalks2@aol.com

Janice Wessman, Instructor
Tel/Fax: (602) 675–8501
wessmanj@aol.com

Harry Zabrocki, Alicia Elliott, Instructors
(602) 538–3046
Hzabro@aol.com

Tucson

Canyon Ranch
John White, Instructor
2025 North Nancy Rose Boulevard
Tucson, AZ 85712
(520) 319–8242

Suzanne Rosin, Instructor
7001 E. Eagle Point Place
Tucson, AZ 85750
(520) 299–0544

Debi Crawford, Instructor
5451 N. Via Del Arbolito
Tucson, AZ 85750
(520) 577–1597
pilatestucson@aol.com

CALIFORNIA

Alhambra (South Pasadena)

Powerhouse
Sasha Koziak, Instructor
1003 Bushnell Street
Alhambra, CA 91801
(626) 458–5600
Koziaks@pacbell.net

Berkeley

Jodie Colone, Instructor
(510) 435–0094
Silverfish76@hotmail.com

Burbank

Merilee Blaisdell, Instructor
(818) 504–9630
MerileeMB@aol.com

Encino

Michael Levy Workout
Michael Levy, Debra Mandis Cozen, Instructors
17200 Ventura Boulevard, #310
Encino, CA 91316
(818) 783–0097
www.venturaboulevard.com/michael-levy

Hacienda Heights

Sharmila Mitra, Instructor
(626) 393–6283
Sharmila44@aol.com

Hollywood

Bill and Jacqui Landrum, Instructors
6315 Ivarene Avenue
Hollywood, CA 90068
(323) 469–2012
jacquilandrum@earthlink.net

Irvine (Orange County)

Audrey Wilson, Angela Ochs, Instructors
5 Bayberry Way
Irvine, CA 92612
(949) 551–3443
Audreydancing.com

Lomita/Torrance

Joellyn Musser, Instructor
24725 Pennsylvania Avenue, C–19
Lomita, CA 90717
(310) 530–7881
clbr8lif@earthlink.net

Los Angeles

It's A Stretch!
Linda Joy Luber, Regina Fox Dawson, Instructors
2130 Sawtelle Boulevard, Suite 207A
Los Angeles, CA 90025
(310) 312–3999
Fax: (310) 312–4999
Itsastretch@juno.com

Regina Fox Dawson, Instructor
(310) 804–5663
regdawson@yahoo.com

Licia Perea, Instructor
2159 Lyric Avenue
Los Angeles, CA 90027
(323) 669–3303
llperea@flash.net

Jennifer Palmer, Instructor
(323) 394–5469

Susannah Todd, Instructor
(818) 625–5488
Susannah13@aol.com

Niedra Gabriel, Instructor
616 N. Spaulding Avenue
Los Angeles, CA 90036
(323) 651–1796

Charlene Hanson, Instructor
1745 Beloit Avenue, #117
Los Angeles, CA 90025
(310) 312–8942

Renda Mishalany, Instructor
332½ N. Orange Grove Avenue
Los Angeles, CA 90036
(213) 525–0293

Miriam Kramer, Instructor
608 S. Dunsmuir Avenue
Los Angeles, CA 90036
(323) 936–1369
Miriamkramer@yahoo.com

Live Art
Anna Caban, Instructor
1100 S. Beverly Drive, Suite 207–208
Los Angeles, CA 90035
(310) 281–7597
www.anacaban.com

Laurel Canyon Studio
Heidi Kling, Instructor
8549 Walnut Drive
Los Angeles, CA 90046
(323) 654–4347
Fax: (323) 654–2396

Kara Springer Wily, Instructor
(323) 933–5875
mlyspringer@reflexnet.com

Heather Cole, Instructor
Hcole123@aol.com

Studio Darien
Darien Gold, Instructor
7507 W. Sunset Boulevard, Suite 14
Los Angeles, CA 90046
(323) 874–2615

Nonna Gleyzer, Instructor
310 S. Hamel, #103
Los Angeles, CA 90048
(310) 385–9485

Karen Biancardi, Instructor
571 N. Gower
Los Angeles, CA 90004
(323) 957–2035
baliraj2@yahoo.com

Malibu

Survival of the Fittest
Jacqueline Berns, Owner and Instructor
3806-J Cross Creek Road
Malibu, CA 90265
(310) 317–0990

Phyllis Reffo, Instructor
30125 Harvester Road
Malibu, CA 90265
(310) 457–8751

Newport Beach

BodyFit
Sheena Jongeneel, Owner and Instructor
Angela Ochs, Instructor
3422 Via Lido
Newport Beach, CA 92663
(949) 675–2639

Lisa May Costich, Instructor
11 Via Florence, #8
Newport Beach, CA 92663
(949) 929–5438
Lisamay98@hotmail.com

Northridge

Melissa Renee, Instructor
19456 Nordhoff Street
Northridge, CA 91324
(818) 772–8900

Oakland

Katherine Davis, Instructor
(510) 832–0653
Kdavis5267@aol.com

Orange

Tiziana Trovati, Instructor
592 N. Pageant Drive, #D
Orange, CA 92869
(714) 771–4416

Pasadena

Zoe
Zoe Hagler, Owner, Instructor, and Teacher Trainer
Merilee Blaisdell, Susannah Todd, Danielle Marcus Janssen,

Instructors
21 South El Molino
Pasadena, CA 91101
(626) 585–8853

Rachel Bhagat, Instructor
rbhagat1@hotmail.com

Redondo Beach

Arlene Renay Reese, Instructor
313 Avenue G
Redondo Beach, CA 90277
(310) 540- 5539

San Diego

Studio Mo
Moses Urbano, Instructor
San Diego, CA 92103
(619) 295–1850 Fax: (619) 295–1023
studiomo@home.com

San Francisco

Golden Gate Studio
Lucero Barry, Instructor
3209 Pierce Street
San Francisco, CA
(415) 637–7919

Catherine Kirsch, Instructor
(415) 288–1001 x 7064
Cherrie_34@hotmail.com

Kerri Palmer Gonen, Instructor
kp_trainer@yahoo.com
Fax: (415) 441–6985

Nancy Rosellini, Instructor
387 Staples Avenue
San Francisco, CA 94112
(415) 441–6985

Jennifer Palmer, Instructor
4135 Cesar Chavez, #14
San Francisco, CA 94131
(415) 517–1044
Palmerpierson@aol.com

Santa Monica

Bodyworks Pilates Conditioning
Nela Fry, Instructor
1008 Euclid Street
Santa Monica, CA 90403
Tel/Fax: (310) 394–2805
Nela@mindspring.com

Heather Leon, Instructor
508A Santa Monica Boulevard
Santa Monica, CA 90401
(310) 394–9780

April Howser, Instructor
(310) 434–9130
Aprilhowser@hotmail.com

Jennifer Bocian, Instructor
(310) 260–9736

Sebastopol

Watta Lee-Ribas, Instructor
613 Sparkes Road
Sebastopol, CA 95472
(707) 823–2879
birthrites@igc.org

Sherman Oaks

Suzi Lonergan–Body Power
Suzi Lonergan, Instructor
(818) 905–6856

ourtney Ca, Instructor
(818) 986–8361
coure@att.net

Trish Garland Studio
Trish Garland, Instructor
13803 Ventura Boulevard
Sherman Oaks, CA 91423
(818) 385–0012
trish_garland@hotmail.com

Valley Village

Danielle Marcus Janssen, Instructor
4950 Laurel Canyon Boulevard, #314
Valley Village, CA 91607
(818) 521–7215
danielle330@earthlink.net

West Hollywood

Winsor Fitness
Mari Winsor, Instructor
945 North La Cienega Boulevard
West Hollywood, CA 90069
(310) 289–8766
Fax: (310) 289–0812

Westwood

Adylia Roman, Instructor
(310) 446–6100 Fax: (310) 446–1128

COLORADO

Boulder

Flatiron Athletic Club
Deidre Szurabajka, Michelle Perkins, Instructors
505 Thunderbird Drive
Boulder, CO 80303
(303) 499–6590
emmaandmichelle@yahoo.com

Breckenridge

Jessica Paffrath, Instructor
(970) 453–2139

Denver

Denver Athletic Club
Amy Halaby, Instructor
1325 Glenarm Place
Denver, CO 80204
(720) 931–6743

Englewood

Body & Mind Awareness
Carlye Flom, Instructor
(720) 989–8585

CONNECTICUT

Colebrook

Eliot Foote, Instructor
(860) 379–9982

Darien

Jeanne Turkel, Instructor
12 McCrea Lane
Darien, CT 06820
(203) 655–1267
Turkel.att.net

Greenwich

Pure Pilates
Mejo Wiggin, Owner and Instructor
Wendy Oliver, Molly Niles, Junghee Kallander, Instructors
(203) 629–3743

Glynis Bylciw, Instructor
(203) 622–1793

Terese T. Garsson, Instructor
58 N. Old Stone Bridge Road
Greenwich, CT 06807
(203) 629–5543
Tgarsson@optonline.com

New Canaan

The Movement Place
Holly Mensching, Cameron Buday, Instructors
11 Burtis Avenue
New Canaan, CT 06840
(203) 972- 3438

Norfolk

Sarah Smolen, Instructor
(860) 542–0081

Ridgefield

Simone Wunderli-Rucolas,
Instructor
124 Tanton Hill Road
Ridgefield, CT 06877
(203) 438–7984
Swisssimi@aol.com

Thomaston

Jeffrey and Sarah Smolen,
Instructors
(860) 283–6428

West Hartford

Elizabeth Flores, Instructor
41 South Main Street
West Hartford, CT 06107
(860) 233–5232

Westport

Bodywork Studio
Christina Bruno,
Ossi Raveh, Instructors
645 Post Road East
Westport, CT 06880
(203) 226–8550

Women's Fitness Edge
Caroline Benton, Instructor
(203) 454–3343 Fax: (203) 454–3342

DISTRICT OF COLUMBIA

Excel Movement Studio
Lesa McLaughlin, Kerry Devivo, Dianne Signiski Garrett, Jill
Kuhlman, Instructors
3407 8th Street, NE, 2nd Floor
Washington, DC 20017
(202) 269–3020

Fitness For Life
Brigitte Ziebell, Instructor
1417 27th Street, NW
Washington, DC 20007
(202) 338–6765

Jennifer Davis Ford, Instructor
2117 Tunlaw Road, NW
Washington, DC 20007
(202) 965–5026
Jen.uine.Pilates@prodigy.net

FLORIDA

Boca Raton

Boca Body Works
Cindy Maybruck, Instructor
7088 Beracasa Way
Boca Raton, FL 33433
(561) 347–1110 Fax: (561) 395–7544
cmaybruck@aol.com

Burnell

Robin Campbell, Instructor
(904) 437–6022

Fort Lauderdale

Alternative Training Studio
David Freeman, Instructor
1517 SE Second Street
Fort Lauderdale, FL 33301
(954) 767–4602
AlternativeTS@aol.com

Martha (Marty) Hammerstein
516 SW 12th Court
Fort Lauderdale, FL 33315
(954) 525–8565

Fort Myers

The Pilates Studio® of Fort Myers
Melissa Derstine, Director and Instructor
11751 Cleveland Avenue, Suites 21 & 22
Ft. Myers, FL 33907
(941) 274–5711
Fax: 941–274–6622

Miami

Teresa Hanson, Instructor
3169 Shipping Avenue
Miami, FL 33133
(305) 205–6292

Orlando

Pilates Mod Bod Studio
Jacki Garland, Jessica Gazzola, Samantha Gazzola, Instructors
8931 Conroy-Windemere Road
Orlando, FL 32835
(407) 903–0641

St. Petersburg

Movement In Motion
Linda McNamar, Instructor
1833 9th Street North
St. Petersburg, FL 33704
(727) 822–4722

Angela Zaun, Instructor
5655A Lynn Lakes Drive South
St. Petersburg, FL 33712
Pilateszaun@hotmail.com

Sarasota

Dynamic Fitness, Inc.
Sherry Resh, Isa Lambert, Christina Bladon-Gadar, Instructors
4141 South Tamiami Trail, Suite 11
Sarasota, FL 34231
(941) 929–9885
S.Resh@aol.com

Winter Park

The Bougainvillea Clinique
Michelle Hartog, R.N., Instructor
4355 Bear Gully Road
Winter Park, FL 32792
(407) 678–3116
mglowhart@aol.com

MatWorkz
Debra Watson, April Aubiel, Instructors
558 W. New England Avenue, Suite 200
Winter Park, FL 32789
(407) 628–4888
www.matworkz.com

GEORGIA

Atlanta

The Pilates Studio® at the Atlanta Ballet
Denise Reeves, Director and Instructor
Robin Warden, Deidra Simon, Emily Bradley, Edgar Tirado,
Lisa Browning, Doris Van Glahn, Instructors
4279 Roswell Road, #208
Atlanta, GA 30342
(404) 459–9555

Studio Lotus
Flo Fitzgerald, Director and Instructor
Nikki Regent, Robin Warden, Emily Bradley, Elizabeth Purdy,
  Instructors
1145 Zonolite Road, Suite 13
Atlanta, GA 30306
(404) 817–0900
www.studiolotus.com

Janet Greenhill, Instructor
4282 Woodland Brook Drive
Atlanta, GA 30339
(404) 351–8032
Jgreenh617@aol.com

Marietta

Core Bodyworks
Lisa Browning, Instructor
1355 Church Street, Ext. #C
Marietta, GA 30060
(770) 231–7849
LBSMT@aol.com

Norcross
The Work
Edgar Tirado, Instructor
5952 Peachtree Ind. Boulevard, Suite 16
Norcross, GA
(770) 518–9610

HAWAII

Makawao

Belkis Lozada, Instructor
Belkis@mauigateway@aol.com

IDAHO

Boise

Forte
Carrie Shanafelt, Instructor
222 North 10th
Boise, ID 83702
(208) 342–4945
Forteboise@earthlink.net

ILLINOIS

Antioch

Patricia L. Kendziora, Instructor
(847) 395–2686

Chicago

Susan Hacker, Instructor
(773) 489–9844

Juanita Lopez, Instructor and
  Teacher Trainer
(312) 878–3639

Julie Schiller, Instructor
1016 North Dearborn
Chicago, IL 60610
(773) 871–2385

Integrations, Inc.
Kevin Bradley, Instructor
1111 North Dearborn, #1905
Chicago, IL 60610
(312) 280–7950 & 8944

David Englund, Instructor
1723 Benson Avenue
Evanston, IL 60201
(847) 866–6190
Mrerolfu@aol.com

Chiropractic Health Resources
Ceci Fano-Bryan, Jacqueline Brenner, Corrine Stanislaw,
  Instructors
2105 N. Southport, #208
Chicago, IL 60614
(773) 472–0560

Pilates Body Design at Flash Fitness USA
Linda Spriggs, Instructor
1470 W. Webster Avenue
Chicago, IL 60614
(773) 325–2100 Fax: (773) 975–9532

Therese Stark, Instructor
(773) 327–4341

Body Endeavors-Performance Gym
Liv Berger, Instructor
1528 N. Halsted
Chicago, IL 60622
(312) 202–0028 Fax: (312) 751–8122
Lsbodydesign@1box.com

Gail Tangeros, Instructor
1720 West Leland #2
Chicago, IL 60640
(773) 561–2854
gtangeros@ameritech.net

Krista Merrill, Instructor
5030 N. Parkside Avenue
Chicago, IL 60630
(773) 545–6165

Susan Hacker, Instructor
(773) 489–9844

Fitness Foundations Chicago
Linda Tremain, PT and Instructor
Krista Merrill, Juliet Cella, Instructors
213 West Institute Place, #303
Chicago, IL 60610
(312) 642–5633 Fax: (312) 642–5733
ktremain@sprynet.com

Juliet Cella Blumenthal, Instructor
2208 W. Farragut
Chicago, IL 60625
(773) 989–8443

Erin Harper, Instructor
5313 N. Ravenswood, #301
Chicago, IL 60640
(773) 989–9979

Andrea Christina Zujko, Instructor
a-zujko@northwestern.edu

Elizabeth Roberts, Instructor
2800 North Lakeshore Drive, Apt. 1302
Chicago, IL 60657–6203
(773) 935–3190
Catlclaw9@yahoo.com

The Pilates Studio® of the Midwest at Hubbard Dance Complex
Julie Dewerd, PT and Instructor
Dana Santi, Manager and Instructor
1151 West Jackson Avenue
Chicago, IL 60607
(312) 492–8835 Fax: (312) 492–8875

Joe Palla, Instructor
5828 N. Paulina
Chicago, IL 60660
(773) 334–6491

Edwardsville

Pam Moody, Instructor
340 South Fillmore
Edwardsville, IL 62025
(618) 692–9763
intbody@plantnet.com

Evanston

The Pilates Studio® of the Midwest
Fatima Bruhns, Director and Instructor
Juanita Lopez, Teacher Trainer and Training Director
Rhonda Celenza, Dana Santi, Joe Palla, Ellen Krafft, Wendy
Madgwick, Randi Neebe, Mary Nardi, Gail Tangeros, Gail
Diehl, Patty Kendziora, Dorota Gottfried, Kirk Gramarossa,
Jill Domke, Instructors
820 Davis Street, Suite 202
Evanston, IL 60201
(847) 492–0464 Fax: (847) 492–0210

Cheryl Ivey, Instructor
1723 Benson
Evanston, IL 60201

Patricia Medros, Instructor
(847) 491–6304
Hwg2948@aol.com

Lady Holly Hathaway, Instructor
2147 Sherman Avenue, #3
Evanston, IL 60201
(847) 864–4318

Glen Carbon

The Integrated Body
Pam Moody, Instructor
23-C Kettle River Drive
Glen Carbon, IL 62034
(618) 656–3890

Glenview

Loribeth Cohen, Instructor
1059 Waukegan Road
Glenview, IL 60025
(847) 657–0881

Highland Park

In Synch Fitness Corp.
Fatima Bruhns, Director and Instructor
Debbie LaMantia, Randi Neebe, Joe Palla, Patty Kendziora,
Allegra Love, Instructors
1898 First Street
Highland Park, IL 60035
(847) 266–1512

Lake Villa

Cathie Derer-McCue, Instructor
38569 Route 59
Lake Villa, IL 60046
(847) 356–0180
CDM HEALTHY BODY@ aol.com

NorthShore

Cheryl Ivey, Instructor
(847) 651–5413
NIY1BERGIE@aol.com

Oakbrook

Fitness Foundations, Inc.
Linda Tremain, PT and Instructor
Jill Popovich, Amy McDowell, Krista Merrill, Erin Harper,
Cindy Venegoni, Instructors
1111 West 22nd Street, #610
Oakbrook, IL 60523
(630) 573–5877 Fax: (630) 573–5875
ltremain@sprynet.com

Oak Park

Alternative Fitness Studio
Andrea Andrade, Instructor
126 N. Oak Park Avenue
Oak Park, IL 60302
(708) 386–4930

St. Charles

Total Body Dynamics, Inc.
Kim Jerrick-Coots, Instructor
2049 Lincoln Highway
St. Charles, IL 60174
(630) 584–2790

Skokie

Barbara Wertico, Instructor
8728 N. Drake
Skokie, IL 60076
(847) 677–7573
BarbWertico@compuserve.com

Willowbrook

Dana Santi, Instructor
6141 Knoll Wood Road
Willowbrook, IL 60514
(630) 654–9834
DanaST919@aol.com

Winnetka

Dorota Gottfried
800 Oak #107
Winnetka, IL 60093

INDIANA

Evansville

Terri Roberts, Instructor

Muncie

Positive Movement
June Hutchinson, Instructor
1411 West Red Maple Road
Muncie, IN 47303–9314
(765) 288–5116
juneh@hr.cami3.com

IOWA

Bettendorf

Gail Diehl, Instructor
4640 Crow Creek Court
Bettendorf, IA 52722–6925
(319) 332–8625

KANSAS

Overland Park

Modern Body Contrology
David Mooney, Instructor
9308 Dearborn
Overland Park, KS 66207
Tel/Fax: (913) 649–1479

LOUISIANA

New Orleans

Uncle Joe's Gym
Larry Gibas, Monica Wilson, Instructors
5008 Prytania Street
New Orleans, LA 70115
(504) 895–5008

MAINE

Belfast

Sustainable Fitness
Beth Tracy, Instructor
96 Main Street
Belfast, ME 04915
(207) 338–2977

Camden

Mo Freeman Teaches
Maureen (Mo) Freeman, Instructor
133 Washington Street
Camden, ME 04843
(207) 230-0073
maureen@mint.net

Portland

Portland Pilates
Nancy Etnier, Instructor
49 Dartmouth Street
Portland, ME 04102
(207) 772-8950

MARYLAND

Baltimore

Goucher College
Elizabeth Lowe Ahearn, Linda R. Moxley, Lynne Balliette, Julie Clime, Jennifer Ellsworth, Instructors
1021 Dulaney Valley Road
Baltimore, MD 21204-2794
(410) 337-6399 Fax: (410) 337-6433
eahearn@goucher.edu

Frederick

Linda Rinier Moxley, Instructor
(301) 694-3015

Hagerstown

Studio Body Logic 2
Karen Garcia, Diane Popper, Instructors
1825 Howell Road
Hagerstown, MD 21740
(703) 991-8343
Snowkysp@msn.com

Kensington

Mary Baily Hash, Instructor
3944 Baltimore Street
Kensington, MD 20895
(301) 942-6855
maryh@lanprovider.com

Mount Rainer

Michael Rooks, Instructor
(301) 927-5127
Rookery@worldnet.att.net

Andrea Chastant, Instructor
(301) 927-2134
achastant@att.net

Takoma Park

RSA Studio
Roberta Stiehm Allen, Instructor
8201 Garland Avenue
Takoma Park, MD 20912
(301) 589-6286
www.Rsastudio.com

Towson

Lynne Balliette, Instructor
269 Ridge Avenue
Towson, MD 21286
(410) 337-6531 x 1
lballiet@goucher.edu

MASSACHUSETTS

Acton

Patrishya Fitzgerald, Instructor
157 School Street
Acton, MA 01720
978-263-9373

Boston

Progressive Bodyworks
Clare Dunphy-Foster, Cheryl Boyle Lathum, Vania Sacramento Delcore, Sarah Faller, Kyra Strasberg
441 Stuart Street
Boston, MA 02116
(617) 247-8090
strongbody@aol.com

Pilates On Centre
Pamela Shore, Instructor
996 Centre Street, #1
Boston, MA 02130
(617) 524-0118
Pshore@quick.com

Gloucester

Joe Porcaro, Instructor
(978) 283-4531

Lenox

Uli Nagel, Instructor
(888) 969-6668

North Weymouth

Fitness Finesse, Inc.
Cheryl Lathum, Instructor
(781) 736-0000

Stockbridge

Mathilde M. Klein, PT and Instructor
21 South Street, Box 1219
Stockbridge, MA 01262
(413) 298-3896

MICHIGAN

Detroit

Nira Pullin, Instructor (for university theater students only)
Wayne State University
Theater Department, 4841 Cass Avenue, Suite 3225
Detroit, MI 48202
(313) 577-3508; (612) 672-6697

Grand Rapids

Jenna and Steve Sisk, Instructors
(616) 540-7376

MISSOURI

Columbia

In Line Studio
Janice Dulak, Owner and Instructor
Amy Higgins-Stambaugh, Instructor
Stephens College Campus
Columbia, MO
(573) 442-2211 x 4715 (studio); (573) 449-0583 (business)
Ahstambaugh@hotmail.com

Amy Higgins-Stambaugh, Instructor
(573) 443-7144

Kirkwood

Susan Bronstein, Instructor
11830 Big Bend Road
Kirkwood, MO 63122
(314) 965-5672 Fax: (314) 965-9317

St. Louis

Kimberly Short, Instructor
534 Warder Avenue
St. Louis, MO 63130
(314) 727-3118
Purepilatesplus@aol.com

Bodies in Balance
Ginger Hedrick, Instructor
2608 Metro Boulevard
St. Louis, MO 63043
(314) 650–7078
Bhedric@mail.win.org

NEW JERSEY

Absecon

Holly's Pure Pilates
Holly Bozzelli, Instructor
119 Marin Drive
Absecon, NJ 08201
(609) 383–8822

Clifton

Madeline Soglin, Instructor
(973) 594–9690
Beaned@aol.com

Englewood

Jeanie Lee, Instructor
(201) 568–0425

Haledon

Julie LoRusso, Instructor
(973) 790–4243
gary-julie@worldnet.att.net

Hohokus

American Body Tech
Kathryn Ross-Nash, Instructor
500 Barnett Place
Hohokus, NJ 07423
(201) 934–9474
bodytech@pipeline.com

Kingston

Integrated Fitness
Donna C. Longo, Instructor
PO Box 44, 4595 Route 27
Kingston, NJ 08528
(609) 252–9229; (609)252–0997

Milltown (Monmouth, Ocean,
and Mercer Counties)

Tori Sikkema, Instructor
17 Trotter Way
Cream Ridge, NJ 08514
(609) 538–4420
Tori@debiz.com

Montclair

Sarah Maria Savia Berger, Instructor
200 Valley Road, #3
Montclair, NJ 07042

Princeton

Anthony Rabara, Instructor
392 Wall Street
Princeton, NJ 08540
(609) 921–7990

Princeton Junction

Marie Snyder, Instructor
(609) 918–9365
Marie-snyder@iname.com

Red Bank

Reform Studio
Kim Lauda, Instructor
The Galleria
2 Bridge Avenue
Red Bank, NJ 07701
(732) 212–0700

Ridgewood

Arlene Dodd, Instructor
75 Wilson Street
Ridgewood, NJ 07450
(201) 445–3102

Teaneck

Energy
Lisa Gratale, Instructor
219 Degraw Avenue
Teaneck, NJ 07666
(201) 836–0457
LisaGratale@msn.com

Tenafly

Hedy Weisbart, Instructor
32 Hillside Avenue
Tenafly, NJ 07670
(201) 541–1677

Titusville

Zane Rankin, Instructor
50A River Drive
Titusville, NJ 08560
(609) 730–9544

Upper Montclair

The Movement Place
Holly Mensching, Cameron Buday, Instructors
48 Northview Avenue
Upper Montclair, NJ 07043
(973) 746–2577

Waldwick

Pamela DeJohn, Instructor
51 Waldwick Avenue
Waldwick, NJ 07463
(201) 652–5986
pamdej@wordnet.att.net

Westmont

Donna M. Tambussi, Instructor
20 Haddon Avenue
Westmont, NJ 08108
(856) 869–3569

NEW MEXICO

Santa Fe

Kathleen Loeks, Instructor
615 Calle de Leon
Santa Fe, NM 87505
(505) 984–2909
Fax:(505) 982–7411
kloeks@cybermesa.com

NEW YORK STATE

Albany

Body Wisdom
Ellen A. Weinstein, Owner and Instructor
Jeanette Sommer, Instructor
344 Fuller Road
Albany, NY 12203
(518) 435–1064

Jeanette Sommer, Instructor
(518) 456–3884
Jette16@Juno.com

Astoria

Angela Ochs, Instructor
(917) 968–0004
Aochs41075@aol.com

Jennifer Holmes, Instructor
35–03 24th Avenue
Astoria, NY 11103
(917) 769–8472
jennifrog76@yahoo.com

Gabrielle Gregori, Instructor
34–27 37th Street
Astoria, NY 11101
(917) 856–2686
indiscipline@earthlink.net

Briarcliff Manor (Westchester County)

Saro Vanasup, Instructor
(845) 762–0040

Brooklyn

Jessica Fadem, Instructor
(718) 469–2265

BodyTonic
Jennifer DeLuca, Instructor
150 5th Avenue
Brooklyn, NY 11217
(718) 622–2755
www.body-tonic.com

Brooklyn Body Control
Rosanna Barberio, Instructor
177 Smith Street, Ground Floor
Brooklyn, NY 11201
(718) 246–2447

Elizabeth Stile, Instructor
(718) 636–5113

Ivanna Wei, Instructor
(718) 783–1750
Dance.on@usa.net

Cold Spring Harbor

Amy Wilson, Instructor
(516) 815–5505

Flushing

Sonia D. Orevillo, Instructor
(718) 321–9069
Soniadomor@aol.com

Glen Cove

Charmian Surface, Instructor
(516) 671–3912

Great Neck

Total Body Dynamics
Patricia O'Donnell, Instructor
(516) 944–0670

Firm 'n' Flex (Northshore Fitness)
Teresa Familio, Instructor
38 Great Neck Road
Great Neck, NY 11021
(516) 466-FIRM

Greenlawn

Mary Lundy Studio
Mary Lundy, Instructor
46 Fenwick Street
Greenlawn, NY 11740
(516) 672–3900

Hastings on Hudson

Bodyscape
Kerry Donegan, Instructor
5 Boulanger Plaza
(914) 478–2639
kerry_bodyscape@hotmail

Huntington

The Pilates Center of Long Island
Maggie Amrhein, Owner and Instructor
Danielle Depass, Jessica Natale, Instructors
15 Green Street
Huntington, NY 11768
(631) 421–1866

Lynn Martens, Instructor
Pinehurst Avenue, #12A
Huntington, NY 10033
lynnemartens@msn.com

The Movement Studio
Terri Safaii, Owner and Instructor
201C East Main Street
Huntington, NY 11743
(631) 549–1400

Irvington

Bella Flex Studio
Nancy Adler, Instructor
(914) 591–5690
adlernm@email.msn.com

Katonah

Equipoise
Carol Dodge Baker, Instructor and Teacher Trainer
Iris Salomon, Instructor
113 Todd Road
Katonah, NY 10536
(914) 232–3689 Fax: (914) 234–9289

Iris Salomon, Instructor
(914) 232–2034
Barnspace@mindspring.com

Kingston

The Movement Center
Leah Chaback Feldman, Instructor and Teacher Trainer
Elise Bacon, Instructor
39 Broadway
Kingston, NY 12401
(845) 331–0986

Lake Placid

Peak Edge Performance, Inc.
Karen Courtland Kelly, Instructor
(518) 523–8706

Mt. Kisco

The Art of Control
Simona Cipriani, Owner and Instructor
Tiziana Trovati, Megan Bridge, Instructors
37 West Main Street
Mt. Kisco, NY 10569
(845) 242–0234

New Paltz

Elise Bacon, Instructor
12 North Chestnut Street
New Paltz, NY 12561
(845) 255–0559

Port Washington

Susan H. N. Brilliant, Inc.
Susan Brilliant, Instructor
405 Main Street, #6
Port Washington, NY 11050
(516) 767–8109

Total Body Dynamics
Patricia O'Donnell, Owner and Instructor
(516) 944–0670

Rhinebeck

The Centering Studio
Deni Bank, Instructor
7 Hook Road
Rhinebeck, NY 12572
(845) 876–5114

Riverdale

Kerri Donegan, Instructor
(718) 548–1175

Rye

Amy Aronson Studio
Amy Aronson, Instructor
560 Polly Park Road
Rye, NY 10580
(845) 921–0522

Saratoga Springs

Lisa Hoffmaster, PT and Instructor
376 Broadway, Suite 5
Saratoga Springs, NY 02866
(518) 677–2557

Scarsdale

Center for Movement
Elle Jardim, Owner and Instructor
Donna Krystofiak, Marta Ferreria, Sonia Orevillo, Jean McCabe,
Kathy Wolfe, Instructors
846 Scarsdale Avenue
Scarsdale, NY 10543
(914) 722–7646

Sleepy Hollow

Saro Vanasup, Instructor
(845) 524–9655

Southampton

Symmetry Studio
Jeanette Davis, Instructor
395 County Road, #39A
Southampton, NY 11968
(631) 204–0122

Suffern

Jennifer Ellsworth, Instructor

Woodbury

Tracy Greenfield, Instructor
(516) 319–4915

NEW YORK CITY

West Side

Anne Walzel, Instructor
(713) 545–7061

The Pilates Studio®
Sean P. Gallagher, PT and Director
Kelly Hogan, Saro Vanasup, Brett Howard, Ton Voogt, Michael
Fritzke, Peter Fiasca, Molly Niles, Sharon Henry, Junghee
Kallander, Brian Eshleman, Kerri Donegan, Cristina Gallio,
Instructors
2121 Broadway, Suite 201 (between 74th and 75th Streets)
New York, NY 10023
(212) 875–0189 Fax: 769–2368

Cynthia Khoury, Instructor
2130 Broadway, #1002
New York, NY 10023
(212) 787–0746

Sharyl Curry, Instructor
1220 Lexington Avenue, #2E
New York, NY 10028
(212) 717–8825

Mathilde M. Klein, PT and Instructor
210 West 78th Street, #3A
New York, NY 10023
(212) 595–3863

Alicia Principe, Instructor
210 West 101st Street
New York, NY 10025
(212) 662–6025

Suzanne Jordan, Instructor
55 West 111th Street
New York, NY 10026
(212) 427–5238
szanjord@usa.com

Jessica Natale, Instructor
(212) 864–2897
Jsnatale@hotmail.com

Heather Snyder, Instructor
(212) 396–9397
Hsnyder2@yahoo.com

Sandra L. Zeuner, Instructor
(212) 663–0688
szeuner@earthlink.net

Christina Richards, Instructor
(212) 362–8939

Junghee Kallander, Instructor
(212) 665–0575
Nabi0@aol.com

Midtown

Drago's Gymnasium
Romana Kryzanowska, Sari Pace, Master Teachers
Daria Pace, Claude Assante, Jennifer Holmes, Instructors
50 West 57th Street, 6th Floor
New York, NY 10019
(212) 757–0724

East Side

Tracy Fiore
215 East 77th Street, Apt. 5A
New York, NY 10021

The Pilates Studio® and Pilates, Inc.
Elyssa Rosenberg, Associate Director
Stephanie Beatty, Suzanne Jordan, Brett Howard, Instructors
890 Broadway, 6th Floor
New York, NY 10003
(800) 474–5283; (888) 474–5283; (212) 358–7676
Fax: (212) 358–7678

Lynne Martens, Instructor
(917) 623–0245
Waybox@aol.com

Premier Physical Therapy & Wellness
Joe Tatta, Instructor
238 East 77th Street
New York, NY 10021
(212) 249–5332

Makiko Oka, Instructor
East 60th Street
New York, NY 10022
(212) 308–0786
Makikooka@aol.com

Geela Roland, Instructor
(212) 754–9071

Julianna Womble, Instructor
320 East 35th Street, #2-H
New York, NY 10016
pilaguru@aol.com
(212) 684–1699

Christy Ann Brown, Instructor
(212) 973–0273

Greenwich Village

Clain Dipalma, Instructor
New York, NY 10011
(212) 229–9369

Alisa Wyatt, Instructor
548½ Hudson Street, #5
New York, NY 10014
(212) 727–1002
Alisawyatt@alisawyatt.com

NoHo

re:AB
Brooke Siler, Owner and Instructor
Daniela Ubide, Jennifer Ruggiero, Amy Wilson, Nikkie Eager,
Ivanna Wei, Maria Hassabi, Frances Craig, Heather Snyder,
Tracy Fiore, Heather Simmons, Lisa Mathison, Instructors
33 Bleecker Street at Mott Street,
   Suite 2C
New York, NY 10012
(212) 420–9111
Fax: (212) 475–4103

SoHo

Halle Markle, Instructor
594 Broadway, #904
New York, NY 10012
(212) 431–8377

Frances Craig, Instructor
(212) 925–4629
Fcraig2@aol.com

TriBeCa

TriBeCa Bodyworks
Alycea Baylis, Owner and Instructor
Elizabeth Knock, Gina Papalia, Hanne Koren, Angeline Shaka,
Alison Thiem, Kathy Buccellato, Tiziana Trovati, Gabrielle
Gregory, Rosanna Barberio, Michele Olson, Sandra L.
Zeuner, Instructors
177 Duane Street
New York, NY 10013
(212) 625–0777 Fax: (212) 625–0030
PilatesNYC@aol.com

Elizabeth Few
ekfew@aol.com

NORTH CAROLINA

Boone

Marianne Adams, Instructor
665 Tarleton Circle
Boone, NC 28607
(828) 262–4991
Adamsm@appstate.edu

Chapel Hill

Celeste Neal Huntington, Instructor
251 S. Elliot Road
Chapel Hill, NC 27514
(919) 929–1536
celestialbodies@mindspring.com

Huntersville

Northeast Health & Fitness
Stephanie Weiner, Instructor
1665 Birkdale Commons Parkway
Huntersville, NC 28078
(704) 895–7048

Wilmington

The Studio
Ben Harris, Instructor
7210 Wrightsville Avenue
Wilmington, NC 28403
(910) 509–1414 Fax: (910) 509–0116

OHIO

Athens

The Body In Mind Studio
Marina Walchli, Leah Jean Rutkowski, Kris Kumfer, Instructors
195 Columbus Road
Athens, OH 45701
(740) 592–6090
walchli@ohiou.edu

Leah Jean Rutkowski, Instructor
11 Hocking St
Athens, OH 45701
(740) 589–6514
LR202595@oak.cats.ohiou.edu

Kris Kumfer, Instructor
(740) 597–6311

Centerville

Body Mind Flex
Cathy Stahura, Instructor
17 N. Main Street, Suite 19A
Centerville, OH 45458
(937) 272–7221

Cincinnati

Pure Fitness, LLC
Pam Medvecky, Instructor
(513) 271–7362
Pamwmed@visto.com

OKLAHOMA

Norman

Laura Wren, Instructor
(405) 321–6171
www.pilatesofoklahoma.com

OREGON

Clackamas

Diane Caldwell, Instructor
(503) 698–4613
dcaldwell@imagina.com

Eugene

Susan Tate, Instructor
(541) 484–4011
State78@hotmail.com

Portland

Studio Adrienne, Inc.
Adrienne Silveria, Diane Caldwell, Instructors
Roxane Murata, Teacher Trainer
614 SW 11th Avenue
Portland, OR 97205
(503) 227–1470
ELN/ro22@earthlink.net

PENNSYLVANIA

Ambler

Peter Fiasca, Instructor
208 Brookwood Drive
Ambler, PA 19002
(215) 205–8004 Fax: (215) 283–9063
pete-f@msn.com

Bryn Mawr

The Pilates Studio® of Bryn Mawr
Megan Egan, Director and Instructor
899 Penn Street
Bryn Mawr, PA 19010
(610) 581–0222 Fax: (610) 581–0223

Doylestown

Physalchemy
Zahra Nasser, Instructor
22 South Main Street, 2nd Floor
Doylestown, PA 18901
(215) 230–0787
Zahra@voicenet.com

Honesdale

Stone Gate Studio
Robin Dodson, Instructor
(570) 251–9408

Newtown

Caroline Nolan Probst, Instructor
(215) 598–8846 Fax: (215) 598–8847
canopro@yahoo.com

Philadelphia

The Pilates Studio® at the P.A. Ballet
June Hines, Megan Egan, Instructors
1101 South Broad Street
Philadelphia, PA 19147
(215) 551–7000 x 1303 Fax: (215) 551–7224

Brie Neff, Instructor
(215) 545–3354
brieadina@earthlink.com

Megan Bridge, Instructor
(215) 925–0244
meganbridge@flashcom.net

Pittsburgh

Christopher Potts, Instructor
820 Maryland Avenue
Pittsburgh, PA 15232
(412) 363–3426

Lynn Rescigno, Instructor
(412) 441–0774

Richboro

Catherine Isaccson, Instructor
1025 Temperance Lane
Richboro, PA 18954
(215) 357–5946
Scicom@bellatlantic.net

Rydal

June Hines, Instructor
1132 Dixon Lane
Rydal, PA 19046
(215) 576–8261

State College

Terri Roberts, Instructor
terriroberts@hotmail.com

Titusville

The Rankin Studio
Zane Rankin, Instructor
50A River Drive
Titusville, PA
(609) 730–9544

Wilkes-Barre

Rose Ann Serpico, Instructor
Rserp@prodigy.net
(570) 824–4391

RHODE ISLAND

East Greenwich

Body Mind Fitness, Inc.
Deborah Montaquila, Instructor
5 Division Street East
East Greenwich, RI 02818
(401) 885–2102

Pawtucket

Patricia Dooley, Instructor
139 Newport Avenue
Pawtucket, RI 02861
(401) 741–8653

Warwick

Pamela Turner, Instructor
(401) 821–5273

SOUTH CAROLINA

Anderson

Edgar Tirado, Instructor
Camp Lou Ann
(864) 226–5439

Columbia

Healing Fitness & Health
Ann Lore, Instructor
128 Woodshore Court
Columbia, SC 29223
(803) 788–7764
angelannsc@webtv.net

TENNESSEE

Franklin

Diane Brignardello, Instructor
(615) 646–2277

Memphis

Bodies In Motion
Sway Hodges, Instructor
5111 Sanderlin Avenue
Memphis, TN 38117
(901) 452–4976

Nashville

Springs Studio
Julie Kraft, Instructor
2021 21st Avenue South, Suite 100
Nashville, TN 37212
(615) 292–1930

Bodies in Balance
Sylvia Gamonet, Grete Teague, Elizabth McCoyd Greer,
  Instructors
5137 Boxcroft Place, 2nd Floor
Nashville, TN 37205
(615) 354–0550
Fax: (615) 354–5107

Grete Gryzwana Teague, Instructor
(615) 321–5100
epiphanydance@mindspring.com

Willow Studio
Bambi Watt, Carrie Chrestman Leal, Instructors
5133 Harding Road
Nashville, TN 37205
(615) 354–1955

TEXAS

Austin

Body Springs Studio
Vicki Hickerson, Instructor
1912 West Anderson Lane, Suite 207
Austin, TX 78757
(512) 452–0115
Fax: (512) 453–8619
www.bodysprings.com;
vicki@bodysprings.com

The Hills Fitness Center
Tracy Anderson, Instructor
4615 Beecaves Road
Austin, TX 78746
(512) 327–4881

Dallas

Body Proof, Inc.
Read Gendler, Instructor
6706 Northaven Road
Dallas, TX 75230
(214) 369–7273
Fax: (214) 369–7990

Houston

Julia Hilleary, Instructor
11100 Louetta, #916
Houston, TX 77070
(281) 257–0001

Anne Walzel, Instructor
1426 Columbia
Houston, TX 77008
(713) 545–7061

UTAH

Orem

Physiques
James Urianza, Instructor
1156 South State Street, Suite 206
Orem, UT 84097
(801) 319–0383
www.Jimurianza@aol.com

Salt Lake City

Body & Mind Studio
Sondra Fair, Instructor
3300 South 1063 East, Suite 201
Salt Lake City, UT 84106
(801) 486–2660

VIRGINIA

Arlington

Studio Body Logic
Karen Garcia, Diane Popper, Simi Nary, Instructors
3017B Clarendon Boulevard
Arlington, VA 22201
(703) 527–9626
Studiobodylogic@earthlink.net

Simi Nary, Instructor
626 N. Jackson Street
Arlington, VA 22201

Forest

Heather Simmons, Instructor
Hmsimmons72@hotmail.com

Leesburg

The Pilates Center, LLC
Chris Abbott, Instructor
504 North Street, NE
Leesburg, VA 20176
(703) 779–7917
Cneabbott@cs.com

Reston

Pure Joe Studios
Michael Rooks, Andrea Chastant, Instructors
2254-M Hunters Woods Village Center
Reston, VA 20191
(703) 860–6766

Richmond

The Pilates Fitness Studio
Jerry Weiss, Pam England, Instructors
2927A West Cary Street
Richmond, VA 23221
(804) 355–5010
jweissguy@juno.com

Virginia Beach

Studio P.
Leslie Vise-Clark, Reid Strasma, Instructors
4020 Bonney Road, Suite 104
Virginia Beach, VA 23452
(757) 306–7007 Fax (757) 306–7009

Axiom
Elyse Tapper Cardon, Instructor
Chambord Commons
332 N. Great Neck Road, Suite 105
Virginia Beach, VA 23454
(757) 486–8665 Fax: (757) 486–8663
davelyse@aol.com

WASHINGTON

Everett

Intrinsic Energy Studio
Bernadette Wilson, Instructor
Isis Wilson, Director of Teacher Training and Instructor
3426 Broadway, Suite 301A
Everett, WA 98201
(425) 252–8240

Kirkland

Atasha Avery, Instructor
Atasha_a@hotmail.com

Redmond

Rebecca Winters, Instructor
(425) 378–7694
contrology@hotmail.com

Seattle

The Pilates Studio® Seattle & Capitol Hill Physical Therapy
Lauren Stephen, Director and Instructor
Lori Coleman-Brown, PT, Director, and Instructor
Anje Marshall, Joe Nicoli, Marywilde Nelson, Sachiko Glass
(PT), ChaCha Guerrero, Danielle Stanky, Teresa Shupe,
Jodie Stolz, Rick Morris, Gay Marcontell, Instructors
413 Fairview Avenue North
Seattle, WA 98109
(206) 405–3560
Fax: (206) 405–3938

Robert Leonard Spa
Christil Siris, Anje Marshall, Rick Morris, Instructors
2033 6th Avenue
Seattle, WA 98121
(206) 441–9900
www.Robertleonard.com

Pilates Center Northwest
Tom Wiseley-Siris, Instructor
501 S. Jackson Street, Suite 305
Seattle, WA 98104
(206) 262–0708
www.Pilatescenternw.com

Rick Morris, Instructor
(206) 898–9189
rikimori@earthlink.net

Dorothee Vandewalle, Teacher Trainer and Instructor
(206) 526–0155

Jennifer Saltzman, Instructor
915 E. Pine Street, #408
Seattle, WA 98122
(206) 726–1903

Shoreline

Peggy Z. Protz, Instructor
102 N. 171st Street
Shoreline, WA 98133
(206) 533–0820
pez009@sttl.uswest.net

WISCONSIN

Milwaukee

Body Mechanics Studio
Jennifer Goldbeck, Instructor
807 N. Jefferson
Milwaukee, WI 53202
(414) 224–8219

WYOMING

Wilson

Interhealth Studio
Sally Baker, Instructor
3465 North Pines Way
PO Box 25204
Wilson, WY 83014–9129
(307) 734–8940
Fax: (307) 733–0391

INTERNATIONAL CERTIFIED INSTRUCTORS

AUSTRALIA

Rozelle

Powerhouse Personal Training
Gina Richter, Chris Lavelle, Marda Willey, Instructors
PO Box 179
Rozelle, NSW 2137
Australia
011–612–9818–6234
Fax: 011–612–9818–6235
powerhouse@hotkey.net.au

Runcorn

Peta Green, Instructor
Petagreen@hotmail.com

Surry Hills

The New York Pilates Studio® of Australia
Cynthia Lochard, Director and Instructor
Roula Kantarzoglou, Edwina Ward, Instructors
Suite 12, Level 4/46–56
Holt Street
Surry Hills, 2010
Australia
Tel/Fax: 011–612–9698–4689
www.pilatesm.com

Sydney

Lisa Mathison, Instructor
Lisamath@hotmail.com

Maria Persenitis, Instructor
17 Macquarie Street
Greenacre, NSW 2190
Australia
011–411–870–468

Victoria

Nexxt Performance Health
Elizabeth Carnegie, Instructor
10 Daly Street
South Yarra, Victoria 3141
Australia
011–613–9804–8111
lizziecarnegie@hotmail.com

AUSTRIA

Vienna

Suzanne McCarty, Instructor
Wiednerhaudtstr 117–41
1050 Vienna
Austria
011–431–545–2049
Mcsuz11@yahoo.com

BERMUDA

Hamilton

Contrology! Bermuda Ltd.
Sophia Cannonier, Lene Danielsen, Hanne Koren, Instructors
48 Parla-Ville Road, Suite 1147
Hamilton, Bermuda HM11
441–291–5895
Fax: 441–236–7998

CANADA

Calgary

Body Dynamics
Lynne Smith, Instructor
924 17th Avenue, SW
Calgary, Alberta T2T0A2
Canada
403–244–4448

Montreal

Deja Griffith, Instructor
3025 Sherbrook Street West, #414
Montreal, Quebec H3Z–1A1
Canada
514–989–8299

Therese Desrosiers, Instructor
Schehera_zade@hotmail.com

Ontario

Symmetria
Michaela Sirbu, Instructor
150 Kent Street
London, Ontario N6A1L3
Canada
519–642–2162
Michaela@symmetria.net

ENGLAND

Cornwall

Gayla Zukevich Stulce, Instructor
6 Meadow Rise
St. Columbus Major
Cornwall TR9 6BL
Great Britain
011–441–637881972
meadowrise@aol.com

London

Daphne Pena Higgs, Instructor
daphnepena@hotmail.com

FRANCE

Paris

Le Studio Pilates de Paris
Phillipe Taupin, Instructor
39, rue du Temple
75004 Paris
France
011–331–427–29174
Fax: 011–331–427–29187
P.Taupin@hotmail.com

GERMANY

Berlin

Galina Rohleder, Instructor
Schluterstr. 13
10625 Berlin
Germany
Tel/Fax: 011–49–30–823–1124

Frankfurt

Leigh Matthews, Mayra Rodriguez de Matthews, Instructors
Hans-Thoma-Str. 7
60596 Frankfurt
Germany
Tel/Fax: 011–49–69–603–2156

Sonthofen

Balance Studio
Rupert Rothmayr, Instructor
Immenstaedter Str.
#13a 87527 Sonthofen
Germany
011–49–8321–788–9222
Fax: 011–49–8321–788–9221
rupertr@t-online.de

Stuttgart

Davorka Kulenovic, Instructor
Sickstr. 32
70190 Stuttgart
Germany
011–497–11–923–9026

GREECE

Athens

Eugenia Papadopolou, Instructor
Corpus Ray, 4 Doxapatri St. 4
114 71 Athens
Greece
011–301–361–7290
Fax: 011–301–361–7290

HONG KONG

Stacy Weitzner, Instructor
Flat B31, 14th Floor
101 Repulse Bay Road
Repulse Bay
Hong Kong
011–852–2812–7948
Fax: 011–852–2812–7973
Pilatesblue@aol.com

ICELAND

Reykjavik

Lisa S.T. Johannsson, Instructor
Suderlandsbraut 12, 3rd Floor
108 Reykjavik
Iceland
011–354–553–0660
Fax: 011–354–557–2948

ITALY

Cagliari

Ass. L'Arte del Controllo
Sara Radici, Instructor
via Roma 59
09100 Cagliari
Italy

Verona

Contrology Studio
Karin Cid, Director and Instructor
Via San Pietro Incamario, 4
37121 Verona
Italy
011–39–0329–2244764
Fax: 011–39–0442–607000
www.contrology-studio.com;
pilates@contrology-studio.com

JAPAN

Tokyo

Yumi Takada, Instructor
University of the Sacred Heart
Hiroo 4 Chome 3–1
Shibuya-Ku, Tokyo
Japan
011–813–548–53884

Makiko Oka, Instructor
2–59–6 Ikebukuro
Toshima-Ku, Tokyo 171
Japan
011–813–984–6546

NETHERLANDS

The Hague

The New York Pilates Studio® of the Netherlands
Marjorie Oron, Owner and Instructor
Jane Poerwoatmodjo. Instructor
Keizerstraat 32
2584 BJ The Hague
Netherlands
011–31–703–508–684
Fax: 011–31–703–228–285
Marjorie@pilates.nl

NORWAY

Oslo

Lene Danielsen, Instructor
lenedani@hotmail.com
011–47–23220080

PORTUGAL

Lisbon

Maria dos Anjos Machado, Instructor
Rua de Angola, blc–6, 3-A
Encosta da Carreira
2750 Cas Cais
Portugal
011–351–148–65652

SPAIN

Barcelona

Estudio El Arte del Control
Javier Perez Pont, Esperanza Aparicio Romero, Instructors
Castanyer 23
Barcelona 08022
Spain
011–349–341–84212
www.artecontrol-pilates.com

Madrid

Estudio Lara
Lara Fermin, Instructor
C/ Magallanes 28, 1 A
28015 Madrid
Spain
Tel/Fax: 011–349–159–43863

SWITZERLAND

Sophie Morabia, Instructor
011–33–450–388195